AIR BORN AGAIN

5-30-2016

A Memoir of Flying and Faith

To My Sister Andrew—
I hope you enjoy the history
of my life. It is with a kind
of fear that I began to write this
venture. Completion — I found it
therapeutic.
Love yes
(Bro)

By Deacon Dennis M. Kudlak
Foreword by Deacon Greg Kandra

Printed in the United States of America

ISBN 978-0-692-70435-6

Library of Congress Control Number: 2016907471

First Edition

14 13 12 11 10 / 10 9 8 7 6 5 4 3 2 1

CONTENTS

FOREWORD

Years ago, someone asked the sister of a priest where she thought vocations came from. She answered without hesitation: "From everywhere!" It's impossible to predict what might spark a desire in someone to be a priest, sister, religious or deacon. The Holy Spirit is endlessly inventive, and you never know who will be called, or how.

And for Exhibit A, look no further than the author of this book, Deacon Dennis Kudlak.

I've often noted on my blog that deacons come from all walks of life, all backgrounds, all upbringings—and Dennis Kudlak proves it. How did a pilot, who regularly found himself touching the heavens, find himself drawn even closer to God?

How did he manage to redirect his life, his faith, his mission? What compelled him to want to serve others

1

as only a deacon can?

You'll have to read this book to find out. It will leave you inspired, uplifted, surprised—and moved.

Dennis's story of conversion and conviction—his journey heavenward, in more ways than one—could be the story of any seeker desiring to draw closer to God. Christianity was built from the fervent faith of doubters who came to believe, of skeptics who came to certainty, and of those in the shadows who found themselves drawn to the light. We are the faith, after all, of Paul and Thomas, Augustine and Ignatius, Francis and Mary Magdalene.

And we are the faith, of course, of Dennis Kudlak.

His story is one more that we need to hear, and what a blessing that the Church is giving him a way to share it, not just in this book but also through his ministry.

The diaconate is a relatively young ministry in the life of the Church; it was restored as a permanent order just 50 years ago. But its impact, especially in the United States, has been nothing less than phenomenal. A good friend of mine has declared that the restored diaconate is one of the great success stories of the Second Vatican Council, and I wouldn't disagree. It has brought a new energy into the Church, and added a new voice to the pulpit: the voice of married men and professionals who bring their own lives and experiences into the preaching of God's Word. Not so very long ago, the notion of a divorced airline pilot proclaiming the Word of God during Sunday Mass would have been unthinkable; the idea of such a person preaching would have been scandalous.

But again: the Holy Spirit is endlessly inventive.

And I invite you to see what I mean by reading the book in your hands. Dennis's journey has much to teach us, and I have no doubt it will be a source of inspiration and hope to many. Who knows? It may even spark one or two people to consider the diaconate.

As Dennis's story teaches us—and as that sister of a priest noted—you can never predict when a vocation might just take off.

Deacon Greg Kandra
Aleteia.org

ACKNOWLEDGMENTS

After contemplating a number of years on writing this book and another year getting the help needed to bring it to completion, the credit for the final product is broad based.

I am greatly indebted to many family, friends and colleagues in making this book become a reality. My best friend and wife of almost twenty-eight years, Lynn Kudlak. My love and appreciation also go to my children, Danielle, Krystal, Mike and Joe for enriching my life in so many ways.

I wish to thank Vaughn Kohler for his invaluable guidance and editing of this project. Thanks to Lorie DeWorken who contributed amazing skill and talent of the interior/exterior design of the book, as well as the upload to Amazon.

Thanks also to Joe Bohrer for approaching me to

write this book. I wish to give a hearty thanks to my friends who read and commented on the manuscript : my friend Bill DiPlacido Jr., Bill DiPlacido Sr., Deacon Tony Alleruzzo, Fr. Larry Richards, Deacon Greg Kandra, Deacon William T. Ditewig, Bishop Donald Trautman. Thank you for your honest response, critique and thoughtful discussions.

I appreciate the spiritual support that I have received in my life for which I am indebted to so many. Most of all, I thank my parents and my sister for a faith formation that I have come to recognize as a priceless gift.

I am grateful to everyone who will read this book and pray that it will be useful in their efforts in searching for God

Finally, I am grateful to God and the Blessed Virgin Mary for their intercessions in my life and helping in bringing this book to its completion.

INTRODUCTION

My View from the Three Seats of My Life

HOW PEOPLE FACE FLIGHT IS DIFFERENT

As a pilot, I found it fascinating how different people respond to flying. Depending on their personality and disposition or even what's happening in their lives at the time, the ways people respond can be radically different. If it's their first time in the air, it's often a mixture of nervousness and excitement. If they suffer from aviophobia—the fear of flying—they are terrified. Others love being up in the air, among the birds and clouds, closer to heaven—so they are delighted. Some don't like airports or flights, so they are just plain—or should I say "plane"—annoyed.

And then there's what I think is the strangest response of all: It's something like disinterest. They seem withdrawn and unconcerned. Here they are roaring across the country at amazing speeds, literally experiencing the miracle of flight. They are experiencing something the vast majority of human beings in the history of this planet have never experienced, and they get the opportunity to look out the window and see majestic mountains and lakes and landscapes and cities from a birds-eye view, and how do they respond?

"Ho hum. I'll go back to reading my magazine."

HOW PEOPLE FACE LIFE IS DIFFERENT

Obviously, people respond to the experience of life in various and very different ways, too. And the emotions are often the same: nervousness, excitement, terror, delight, and yes, disinterest, withdrawal, and boredom. Just like passengers may respond differently to flying based on where they are sitting in the plane—front or back, aisle or window seat—so people respond to life based on "where they are sitting." They are "looking out the window" from a certain perspective and it makes all the difference in how they see things.

HOW I FACE EVERYTHING: MY THREE "SEATS"

As of the printing of this book, I am 66 years old. I grew up, and have lived, in Erie, Pennsylvania my whole life. And for the duration of my flight here on earth, I have seen the world from mainly three different perspectives. You might call them "three seats" from which I have viewed all of life—and *my* life.

SEAT ONE: ON A WING...

The first seat I already alluded to. For forty-seven years of my life, I have been a pilot.

I got started in aviation from my parents. My dad was a pilot in World War II and in 1946, after the war he, along with his two brothers, started an aviation business called Erie Airways. By 1983, Erie Airways was one of the largest fixed-base aviation operations in the Northeast. We had over 13 aircraft and twenty pilots.

When I was sixteen, like most teens I was excited about getting my license. But unlike most teens, I wanted a license to fly more than a license to drive. I was far more interested in flying and successfully completed my first solo flight on August 7th, 1966. My dad was my flight instructor and my uncle was the F.A.A. designated flight examiner.

For a little while in high school, I became more interested in playing sports and thought less of flying. But by the time I graduated from college, and as I looked around for job opportunities, becoming a pilot really interested me. I graduated from Gannon College with a degree in business, but after having some entry-level business employment, I realized that aviation was in my blood. So I pursued all my airplane ratings and stated my flying career with Jetstream International Airlines (which was started in my hometown of Erie, PA). I flew with them for five years until I got hired by Continental Airlines in 1988.

TWENTY-SIX YEARS IN THE SKY

On July 23, 2014, I retired after twenty-six years with the same company and forty-seven years of working life. At 1:00 in the afternoon, I left the terminal building where I had been based for the past twenty-one years, said good-bye to my chief pilot, the union personnel, and quietly walked away.

I had mixed emotions but was calm and didn't meet anyone as I departed the terminal building, which is lucky since I doubt my calmness would have held-up. For twenty-six years, I had given my life to this company and it too had given me life—not just an opportunity for employment, salary, and a pension, but the chance to do what I wanted to do with my life, to be the kind of individual I wanted to be and to be happy at what I was doing. I am very grateful for the times I spent there. I did feel funny knowing that I would never again pilot a commercial airline, but the decision to retire from the airline industry was made by the age restrictions of Federal Aviation Administration. (I believe that I could have been an airline pilot for several more years.)

As a pilot, you are part of a select group of Americans. Less than one-third of one percent of us know how to fly an airplane. That makes you unique. After you have tasted flight, you will forever walk with your eyes turned skyward and long to return too.

SEAT TWO: AND A PRAYER...

I am also a permanent deacon in the Catholic Church. This is also a unique "seat" to occupy in life and it has provided me with a unique perspective. A friend of mine, who is also a permanent deacon, said recently that he spends most of his time tucked between the priesthood and the laity, serving both but different from both. It's a special vocation, and it calls for unusually mature and committed men. (That sometimes makes me wonder how I got to become one!) But my friend is right. Deacons, like priests and bishops, belong to the clergy. They're no longer laymen. In fact, all priests and bishops, including the Holy Father, remain deacons, even as they are ordained into the priesthood or episcopacy. (They also, obviously, remain part of the baptized faithful.)

But a permanent deacon, as opposed to a "transitional" deacon preparing for priesthood, will also frequently have a wife, children and a regular job. In most ways, permanent deacons share the same joys and sorrows as any layperson. We may know these men as our married neighbors, soccer coaches, fathers, or co-workers at the office.

Deacons receive the sacrament of orders, to the Order of Deacons, when a bishop lays hands on them and prays a prayer of consecration. Just as in baptism and confirmation, deacons receive an indelible character, marking them forever and enabling them to live in a specific configuration to Christ. They receive special sacramental graces to assist the "bishop and his priests as ministers of the word, of the altar, and of charity."

Deacons may seem new since Vatican II, but they actually trace their ministry to the earliest days of the Church in Jerusalem. In the Acts of the Apostles, deacons were called to assist the apostles through works of charity. In fact, the Greek root of the word "deacon"—*diakonos*—means "servant." Saint Stephen, the first Christian martyr, was a deacon, as was Saint Philip, who is known for evangelizing the Ethiopians.

The identity of the deacon is not solely associated with his function of being a servant but more so with his spirituality rooted in his ordination to the Order of Deacons and his connection and obedience to his bishop and the bishop's successors. A foreshadowing of the office of deacon in the Church predates the New Testament. In the Book of Numbers, the Prayer of Ordination for deacons the "sons of Levi" are recalled.

The Church teaches that service, *diakonia*, is grounded in the Gospel and expressed best in the first sacrament of baptism. The mandate given to the apostles by Jesus is summed up in Matthew 18 when he says to them, "All power in heaven and on earth has been given to me. *Now go...*" Christian service is understood and modeled from the ministry of Jesus, which is to do the will of the Father. This is the *diakonia* of the Father that is handed down to the apostles and through apostolic succession to the bishops and, by the laying on of hands, to priests and deacons. The deacon, who comes from the bishop and belongs to the bishop, exemplifies the *diakonia* of the Father through the ministry of the bishop as the true Shepherd of His flock.

I've had some pretty amazing experiences as a deacon. And they've allowed me to view life in a unique way.

SEAT THREE: ...AND CAUGHT IN THE GEARS OF LIFE

The final seat I've worn, and the perspective I've been able to have, is not rare at all. It's one that a lot of people have occupied. It's the seat of suffering, of being a human being who has been, time in and time out, caught in the gears of life. Compared to a lot of people, my troubles haven't been that bad. But I have had troubles—and some of them were a result of decisions I made.

When I was very young, my younger sister died of a horrible disease. The death rocked the life—and faith—of my family. I went into a depression and associated with indecent and immoral activities and people. I've also had financial issues and family drama—just like a lot of people.

So I understand when other people struggle—not just at succeeding in life, but in living in the presence of God, which is so life-changing.

BLESSED TO BE IN THESE SEATS

The thing is, I feel incredibly blessed to have been able to occupy these three seats in life. Whether as a pilot, a deacon, or a broken human being like everyone else, I feel like I have learned so much about life, faith, and God. I believe that my career in aviation, my ministry as a deacon, and my tough experiences in life, have all taught me incredible lessons. So I wanted to draw on my perspective and experiences to help you live your life better and draw closer to understanding God and his ways.

NOT A HEAVY BOOK, BUT HEART-FELT

I did get formal theological training for my ministry as a deacon. I read and pray with Scripture daily, along with studying the Catechism of the Catholic Church. But this will not be a book that is heavy in theological knowledge or philosophy. One of my favorite theologians, Karl Rahner, once said, "The Christian of the future will be a mystic, or he will not be a Christian at all." Simply put, a mystic isn't someone who just knows things about God. He or she is someone who knows God in real, heartfelt experience, through prayer and encountering God in different situations in real life. Mystics come to have intimacy with God and learn his ways through the things that actually happen on a day-to-day basis. They come to really know and love God through the actual story of their lives.

SHARING MY STORY—AND STORIES

With this in mind, that's what I want to do: I want to share the story of my life—and stories from my life—where I encountered God or learned a lesson he wanted to teach me. It's my hope that you wouldn't just grow in information about God, but that you would grow closer to God himself through what I am going to share.

Life is like irreversible gears, only moving in one direction, and we carry with us a lot of baggage.

Let me put it this way: As a pilot, I took people on flights. With this book, I want to take you on one man's journey of faith and growing closer to God. As a deacon, I help people and often share important lessons of faith. Through this book, I want to help you with the lessons that God has taught me in my life. And as a human being who has experienced his share of trials and suffering, I just want to encourage you. God will not protect you from all pain, but he can redeem it. Jesus is the King of Kings, but he first endured the cross. Above all, I want to help you believe that "all things work together for the good of those who love God" (Romans 8:28).

Are you ready? Welcome aboard, fasten your seatbelts, and prepare for take-off!

CHAPTER ONE

In the Beginning...
Was an Airport

I f you were to talk to a Hall of Fame basketball player, you wouldn't be surprised if he told you that he grew up spending every waking moment at the gym. You wouldn't be surprised if a famous biologist grew up as the son of a ranger and spent his childhood running through the forest of Yosemite National Park. You wouldn't be surprised if a famous chef spent his childhood in a restaurant, the son of a restaurateur.

The places we grow up, the buildings we spend time in—a lot of time—shape our future. They influence what we do in life and who we become.

For me, that place is an airport. Specifically, the Fairview Airport in Erie, Pennsylvania.

FIRST FLIGHT

You might think that a man who was born into a family

of aviators might take his first flight with his dad or one of his brothers. Not so in my case. According to my friend Joe Bohrer, he was the first person to take me up in a plane. It wasn't exactly a smooth, care-free ride.

According to Joe, I was about two or three years old when my dad approached him one late Friday afternoon and asked him if he would mind taking me up for a quick ride around the airport in Fairview, Pennsylvania.

Joe admitted to me that he was a bit surprised by the question—and his surprise turned quickly to fear and suspicion. Why would my dad ask him to take me up? Why didn't my own father take me up? These were some of the questions running through his mind—and when I got older, I wondered the same thing.

Well, regardless of his confusion, Joe reluctantly agreed and took me up. When I talked to him about my first flight, he told me that his "guardian angel" must have been with him on that day. That got my attention and I asked him to explain.

"Being a newly licensed pilot, I didn't have much experience," he said. "And on that day, the sun was just setting and I had a difficult time adjusting to the glide path of the grass runway."

Joe proceeded to tell me that his approach to the runway was a bit fast, and he landed a bit long. So, when he touched down, he didn't think he would be able to stop at the end of the fast approaching runway. But he did get the aircraft stopped right at the very end of the strip.

"While we were taxiing back to the office, I thought your dad was going to question me about my approach and landing," he said. "But he didn't."

Personally, I think that my dad knew that Joe was a very responsible and safe pilot and wanted to show Joe that he trusted him talking his son up. Even though he struggled with the approach and landing, I'm sure my dad's trust boosted his confidence.

There are many times in life when we lack confidence. We wonder if we can really handle the challenges we face. My dad honored Joe by placing the safety of his son in his hands. Jesus placed his trust in his father when he was being crucified, saying "Father, into your hands I commit my spirit" (Luke 23:46). We honor God when we follow his son and trust him, too.

FOND MEMORIES OF FAIRVIEW

I spent a lot of time at the Fairview Airport with my dad, sister, and uncles. I still have some fond memories. My fondest memories are the times I spent with my sister at the airport. She was two years younger than me and we enjoyed going in and out of the three hangars; looking into all the different planes, riding the lawn mowers, and playing with the two "airport dogs," Rudder and Torque.

MY OWN SOAP OPERA

Of course, life is full of both good and bad. I do have some unpleasant memories of the airport, too.

One of my most unpleasant experiences came when I was inside one of the airplanes. My dad had told me it was okay to be in an airplane, but I was *never* to touch anything.

Kids being kids, I did touch some things in the airplane that I wasn't supposed to. Unbeknownst to me, I accidently turned on the battery power of the airplane, along with one of the radios, and started to talk into the airplane's microphone. I started to transmit some cuss words over the aircraft's radio, which were heard over the office radio receiver, and people started a frantic search for me.

There must have been over thirty-five airplanes in the hangar, but it didn't take long for my uncle Joe to locate me in an Aeronca Champ and extricate me from the airplane. I was quickly escorted to the office, where my dad was waiting for me. My dad took me outside and told me how displeased he was that I didn't listen to his specific requirements regarding playing around the airplanes and hangars. He was also deeply disappointed by the profane language coming from his little boy's mouth.

Apparently, I had done this before and was only given a stern warning; but this time my dad wanted to make sure that he would leave a lasting impression on me (which he did). He decided to put soap in my mouth and make me sit on the bench outside the office.

I don't remember how long I sat there with soap dripping from my mouth, but it seemed like an eternity.

As I recall, the soap wasn't that unpleasant. What was unpleasant was hearing the comments from all the people who entered the office and observed my bent head with soap dripping out-of-it.

From that day on, I never went into another airplane as a kid nor said a cuss word. When I tell that story to friends and my family, I receive a common response: "how cruel" that was for my dad to do that. I don't believe that it was the best method my dad could have selected. But I do know that I preferred getting spanked to getting soap in my mouth. I used to think that I hated my dad after the "soaping" but that stopped after two soap snacks.

That incident—and others like it—linger in my mind and remind me of the way it is with life. We have unpleasant things happen to us. But very often, those unpleasant things are the result of choices we make and actions we take.

ERIE'S AIRPORT AND THE EVERLASTING GOD

At the end of the First World War, civil aviation in the United States was primarily unregulated and mostly made-up of "Barnstormers," which were pilots operating expensive military surplus aircraft from city-to-city. They would openly land in farm fields on the outskirts of town as airports were very scarce at that time.

The Air Commerce Act of 1926 enacted laws that raised the standards for ensuring passenger safety. As these laws began to take effect, the transient nature of the industry changed into what was called a "Fixed Base Operation." In general, we usually think of a Fixed Base Operation at or adjacent to an airport where general aviation, business, or private aircraft operate. But today the term is used to define any commercial enterprise that has permits to operate at an airport and provide services. As of April 2009, the number of FBO's operating in the United States was estimated at 3,138.

After the war, Erie County Flying Service fell into serious disrepair. In 1946, Mike Andy and Joe Kudlak purchased the property and built two more hangars and an administration building calling their operation Erie County Flying Service. It soon became a major flight center for flight instruction, charter service, air shows, and air races on the weekends. It was not unusual to have a crowd of 3,000 show up. People from all over the world would come to the airport to be entertained by the air show or just watch the take-offs and landings.

In 1957 Erie County Flying Service had grown to a point where the business needed to operate out of an airport with hard surfaced runways and an instrument landing system. In November of 1957, the Kudlak brothers moved their business to Port Erie Airport. That Fixed Base Operation was named Erie Airways, Inc. A year later, they sold their Fairview property and moved their entire operation to Port Erie Airport.

The history of aviation in America is a microcosm of all of life. Over time, the old ways pass on, new ways of doing things develop. Planes crash. Buildings rise from the ground. Everything either adapts or dies. From the very first Barnstormers of the early 1900s to the pilots of the Airbus A380, the biggest commercial aircraft in existence today, a lot of time has been spent in the air—and a lot of sand has passed through the hourglass. How comforting, then, to know the words of Psalm 90:1:

> *You have been our dwelling place in all generations.*
> *Before the mountains were born or you gave birth to*
> *the earth and the world,*
> *Even from everlasting to everlasting, You are God.*

SATISFIED WITH A LIFE IN THE SKY

My Dad, Michael Kudlak, used to tell me that the airport is one of those things that make a community "whole." It's like a hospital, he said, or a church. I believe he was right back then. I think his words still ring true today.

I don't know where you grew up. I don't know what places have defined what you have done in your life or who you are. But there's no question your environment has shaped you in ways that perhaps you've never thought of. It has shaped your view of history, the world, God, your family, and even you. It might be good to spend a little more time thinking about that.

I cannot imagine growing up without the memories that I have of planes and flying and the Fairview

Airport. My very experience of life is inseparable from my time spent in airport towers and hangars. So many of the analogies that I use to understand God and his ways and the life of faith, hope, and love are drawn from flying.

A life associated with the sky has been a rich, satisfying life. Hopefully, it has prepared me for that day when I will go up to meet the Lord in Heaven. In any case, I am very thankful for this life that I have been given.

CHAPTER TWO

Words That Hurt, Help, and Make You Holy

³¹The Jews took up stones again to stone him.³²Jesus answered them, "I have shown you many good works from the Father; for which of these do you stone me?"³³The Jews answered him, "It is not for a good work that we stone you but for blasphemy; because you, being a man, make yourself God."³⁴Jesus answered them, "Is it not written in your law, 'I said, you are gods'?³⁵If he called them gods to whom the word of God came (and scripture cannot be broken),³⁶do you say of him whom the Father consecrated and sent into the world, 'You are blaspheming,' because I said, 'I am the Son of God'?³⁷If I am not doing the works of my Father, then do not believe me;³⁸but if I do them, even though you do not believe me, believe the works, that you may know and understand that the Father is in me and I am in the Father."³⁹Again they tried to arrest him, but he escaped from their hands. ⁴⁰He went away again across the Jordan to the place where John at first baptized, and there he remained.⁴¹And many came to him; and they said, "John did no sign, but everything that John said about this man was true."⁴²And many believed in him there.

JOHN 10:31-42 (Revised Standard Version)

In John's Gospel, Jesus speaks powerful words. He teaches the crowd about himself and explains, in a somewhat roundabout way, that he is God. He says, "I am the Way, the Truth, and the Life" (John 14:6). In the tenth chapter, some of the Jewish leaders hear his words and are infuriated by them. They say he is guilty of blasphemy: "You, a man, are making yourself God." In response to this, they pick up rocks to stone Jesus (John 10:31-42).

Thank goodness, we have evolved as a civilization. At least in America, we don't literally throw rocks at people with whom we disagree. But I think a stone is a great metaphor for words. Just like stones, words are powerful objects. You can use them to build a wall that serves a good purpose. Or you can use them to kill someone. In the same way, words can be used to draw us closer to God. They can be used to heal and encourage. Or they can be used to hurt and destroy.

The experiences I've had in my life have taught me a lot about this.

WORDS THAT LEAD TO MIRACLES

When I was about four or five-years-old, my mom went to the hospital for surgery on her goiter. She said that her neck was quite swollen and at the urging of her sister, Sophie, she went to see her physician.

Preliminary tests showed that it was malignant and needed to be extracted. The night before the surgery, my aunt Sophie visited my mom and gave her a statue of the Infant Jesus of Prague and told her to pray for his intercession that the removal of her goiter would be successful.

That night, my mom prayed for the intercession of the Infant Jesus and around 4:00 in the morning, the nurse came into the ward to prep my mom for surgery. My mom said the nurse felt around her neck for a few minutes then made a gasp and ran out of the ward. A few minutes later, she returned with a physician who also checked her neck area and then he abruptly left, but returned moments later with two other physicians.

This time, they turned on the lights in the entire ward —which woke everybody up—and examined my mom, asking her many questions. The goiter was gone! Before they released her from the hospital, one of the physicians asked her if she had any idea what just occurred. My mom replied, "last night, I prayed to the Infant Jesus of Prague for his intercession and my prayers were answered." They told her that there was nothing for them to do and that she could go home. The memory of that event is the strongest memory I carry with me about my mother.

Of course, her healing was a miracle, a moment of real joy in a life that was otherwise full of trials and difficulties. Since my dad and two brothers were building up their flying business, he spent six days a week, seventy-two hours, at work—although it was still imperative that my dad had Sundays off so we could all attend Mass as a family. But basically, my mom took on the responsibility of raising me and my sister. I'm sure it was tough.

Even so, she was strong, because her journey of faith and human growth revolved around her regular attendance at Mass and her prayer life. Remember when I mentioned what Karl Rahner said about mystic Christians? They know God in real experience, in real relationship. In that sense, my mom was a mystic. The words she spoke in prayer drew her closer to God. Those same words also resulted in blessings for others. Through prayer, my mom's journey with God and her deepest held values became a shared journey with our family and contributed to my learning so much about life and faith.

WORDS THAT LEAD TO TEARS

But not all words bring healing. I learned this when I was still very young.

For all intents and purposes, I had a typical child-hood. I grew up a part of a working-class family. Throughout my childhood, we lived in a stable suburb of a small city. I remember going over to my grandpar-ents' house on Christmas Eve and after midnight Mass we would gather at their house for a meal.

At some point during the visit, I always would fall asleep. As I recall, I would always wake up in my bed on Christmas Day, not remembering how I got there. I know that my parents were concerned about my aca-demic progress in school, specifically kindergarten. According to my mom, the nun at St. Mary's informed them that I may have to repeat kindergarten because I was not participating in class.

My parents were devastated. My mom began a Novena to the Infant Jesus of Prague. My dad thought this nun was not accurately assessing my lack of "enthu-siasm" for kindergarten, so he took me to a psychol-ogist for an evaluation. After several hours of testing, the psychologist returned with his assessment of me: "There is nothing wrong with your son. He's just a bit lazy." I did not have to repeat kindergarten, after all. My mother was overwhelmed and thanked God for her prayers being answered.

While I struggled academically, my younger sis-ter was a genius. Learning came easy to her and she always earned straight A's. She definitely received the "smart gene" from my dad. In spite of this difference in

IQ, my sister and I were very close.

I benefitted so much from my relationship with her. I was a premature baby and developed rheumatic fever when I was about five or six. Because of this, I was a frail, underweight child and a number of boys in the neighborhood singled me out to bully. They called me names. It hurt—a lot.

My parents used to tell me to tell the bullies that "sticks and stones may break my bones, but words will never hurt me." But that didn't help. It was not uncommon for me to come home crying because some of the boys tied my shoe strings together and pushed me around while I tried to untangle them.

My dad wanted me to stick-up for myself and fight my own battles. He very seldom came to my rescue and prevented my mom from coming to my aid. So the person who did come to my aid was my sister. That's right: A young girl *who was two years younger than her brother*. She feared no one.

One day is still clear in my memory: I was outside playing and one of my playmates tied my shoe strings together and started popping me on the head. I started to cry and scream for help. Before I knew it, I heard my sister come running out of the house, screaming, "You leave my brother alone!"

Immediately, she confronted two of the bullies and started physically engaging them. After just a couple of minutes, both of them ran away—and never teased me again. I was very grateful for my sister's intervention, but I asked her not to tell dad, because I knew he would have been disappointed that I couldn't defend myself. We had a strong bond and I really felt proud to be her brother.

Of course, those kids who teased me were not hurtling actual rocks at me. But their words still stung. At the time, they did major damage to me, even though no bruises were made or blood spilled. Thankfully, my little sister countered with words of correction for them and words of encouragement for me.

BETTER BELIEVE WORDS WILL HURT, HELP, OR MAKE YOU HOLY

"Sticks and stones may break my bones, but words will never hurt me." No doubt about it, that old saying got it wrong. It underestimated the power of words. As I've learned in my own life, words can be devastating or positively beneficial and strengthening. My experience is supported by Sacred Scripture. Some of the more weighty texts in the Bible are reserved for teachings about our tongue: "Let no evil talk come out of your mouths, but only what is useful for building up," St. Paul says in Ephesians 4:29. In fact, the Bible goes so far as to say in Proverbs 18:21 that "the tongue has the power of life and death."

How have you been impacted—positively or negatively—by the power of words? How do you impact others with what comes out of your mouth?

CHAPTER THREE

My Sister's Suffering, Scratches, and the Savior's Love

During the years I grew from a small child into a teenager, life was very intense. It provided more than a few opportunities to grow as a person—physically, emotionally, and intellectually. That growth was not without its growing pains, because this era in my family's life was characterized by upheaval and confusion.

Experts say the teen years are a time when young people seek to gain more independence. To do this, they start pulling away from their parents—especially the one they are closest to. During this phase, it seems like teens are always at odds with their parents and don't want to be around them the way they used to. This was definitely true for me. It was not true for my sister Joyce.

For me, going from elementary school to an all-male Catholic high school felt like I was starting all over again. My sister was only one year behind me, and she also made the transition from elementary school to Villa Maria, an all-female Catholic high school. We both had to meet new people, make new friends, and learn to balance schoolwork and extracurricular activities. I found it really tough. But for her, it was easy.

THE SUFFERING OF MY SISTER

However, during her freshman year at Villa, my sister experienced something that wasn't easy at all. Quite the opposite. She began to experience the same recurring illness every three months. Her symptoms included a high temperature and frequent vomiting. My mother would take her to the doctor's office and he would always diagnose it as the flu.

Her condition persisted until eventually my sister experienced these same symptoms on a monthly basis. Finally, my dad told my mom to take her to another doctor for a second opinion. My mom received a second opinion, a diagnosis that was far more serious: Joyce was suffering from a severe kidney disease. The months of high temperatures without treatment destroyed my sister's one kidney and caused her other kidney to be only 35% effective. The doctor told my parents that she needed a kidney transplant right away, and recommended that she start kidney dialysis twice a week until a kidney became available. Unfortunately, Joyce also had a rare blood type, AB+. So the doctor said it could take a while to get a match for the transplant.

Dr. Robert Lasher was one of the first doctors to develop a kidney dialysis machine at Hamot hospital in Erie, Pennsylvania. My sister had to go to that hospital twice a week to undergo the procedure that would clean her blood. It wasn't a quick treatment. It took approximately nine hours. She would leave school at 4:30 and immediately go to the hospital, where she would do her homework while on dialysis. When the dialysis procedure was over, it left her feeling very sick, tired, and it always took her a day or two to completely recover. The doctor told my parents that if she didn't receive a kidney transplant within a couple of years, her bones would become brittle and susceptible to breakage.

Obviously, this was an extremely difficult situation for my sister. Yet I wasn't acutely aware of the seriousness of her condition. I was a seventeen-year-old boy during this time and was involved and committed to sports and girls. I took it for granted that she would be on dialysis for a short time and eventually be cured. My parents never sat me down and explained her situation or her long-term prognosis.

On June 23, 1966, it was discovered that my sister had suffered complications from her dialysis procedure. During one of her earlier treatments, a mistake had been made disconnecting her from the machine and her blood had become contaminated. As a result, she was admitted to the hospital. The next day, the doctors determined that my sister needed a complete blood transfusion right away. Immediately, a search began to obtain her rare blood type.

That same evening, something happened I will never forget. My parents were already in bed for the night. My dad had fallen asleep immediately, but my mom was awake working on a crossword puzzle. I had gone to bed early and fell asleep immediately.

It was a warm summer night and my mom had the bedroom windows open. Just past midnight, a scratching noise on the bedroom screen startled my mom. She recoiled in her bed and whispered my dad's name to get his attention. She made two more attempts with no success. Then, just as suddenly the scratching noise began, it stopped. After a few moments, my mom calmed down and returned to her crossword puzzle.

About three minutes later, the scratching on the bedroom screen returned. This time my mom yelled at my dad to wake up.

"What's the matter?" he asked.

"There is someone scratching on the bedroom screen," she said.

"Go to sleep," he answered. "It's probably just a bird."

Shortly after saying this, the scratching on the screen stopped.

A few minutes after that, the phone rang. My dad jumped up and answered the phone. It was the hospital informing my dad that my sister's condition had turned for the worse and that they needed to get down to the hospital right away.

My mom and dad got dressed in a hurry. Before they rushed out of the house, my dad knocked on my bedroom door, woke me up, and told me that I should come with them to the hospital because my sister was gravely ill.

"She'll be fine," I said, half asleep. "I'm going to stay here."

I'm not sure how much time elapsed from the time my parents left the house. All that I remember is that I was in a deep sleep when "something" or "someone" woke me up and told me to get to the hospital now. I immediately got dressed and drove to the hospital. I remember feeling very uneasy during my drive; and when I arrived at the hospital, I rushed to my sister's room, but wasn't expecting to see a nurse stripping the sheets off her bed.

"Can I help you?" she asked me.

"Yes," I said. "I'm looking for my sister, Joyce Kudlak."

She gave me a sympathetic look.

"Oh, I'm sorry son," she said. "She's moved on."

"What?" I asked. "Where did she go?"

I didn't understand what she meant. *Where is she?* I needed to see her.

"I'm really sorry," the nurse said. "She is deceased."

I felt my body going numb. I told the nurse I wanted to see her, but she said that was impossible because her body was already at the morgue. I turned around and started walking, aimlessly, like a zombie, trying in vain to locate the morgue. I wandered out to the parking lot, got in my car, and drove around for hours in a catatonic state. Finally, I returned home and mourned with my parents and a couple aunts and uncles.

"Are you okay?" my dad asked me. "Do you want to talk about it?"

"No," I said.

I just wanted to be by myself. I went to my bedroom and wept for hours.

THE FINGERS OF A FAITHFUL GIRL

When we arrived at the funeral home for the viewing, my dad, mom, and I were given a private moment to be with my sister before the public viewing began. I was still in disbelief, and seeing my sister in the casket was surreal. After several minutes of reflection and prayer, my mother became very upset and demanded to see the funeral director.

"What's the matter?" my dad asked her.

"Look at her right hand!" she answered through tears.

We both looked at my sister's right hand, but didn't see anything out of the ordinary. But my mother became even more incensed and marched out of the room and summoned the funeral director. When he arrived, my mother asked him to explain why my sister's fingernails on her right hand were split and distorted.

"We didn't do anything to her nails," he said. "They were in that condition when she arrived from the hospital."

Impossible, we thought. My sister had beautiful long nails and she was very conscientious about their appearance. Plus, her fingernails on her left hand were perfect. My dad and I didn't make a big deal about it and didn't understand why my mom was so upset.

It wasn't until later, during my sister's wake, that all three of us started to go over the events of her last night with us. Eventually, we realized that my sister had said goodbye to us in a way that was spiritual, incredible, and beautiful. As we recalled the details surrounding her final moments, we realized that the scratching sound that my mother had heard were almost immediately followed by the call from the hospital and coincided with the exact time my sister left us and passed into Eternity.

But the story gets even more amazing. Archbishop Gannon, along with a number of the Sisters of Saint Joseph, attended my sister's funeral and told my mother and father something incredible: A month before she passed, Joyce told several of the nuns that they would experience a significant event, one that no one could predict without divine assistance. Her revelation came true. That event came to fruition a week before my sister passed. When Joyce's prediction came true, the nuns immediately informed Archbishop Gannon. He then relayed the message and told them something extraordinary.

"I believe," he said. "That your daughter is a saint."

Later on in life, some things happened that supported the notion that my sister was a saint. Forty-five years after my sister's passing, a friend of ours named Linda Samillo called me with a message. She told me that she was hesitant to share it with me for fear I'd think she was unstable. But she felt like she needed to. She told me that my sister Joyce wanted Linda to tell me that Joyce was "fine and doing well." And that I should "not worry about her."

Admittedly, I was a little confused. Why wouldn't Joyce communicate that message to me directly—by herself? Why go through another person? But our priest friend Father Pete thought it made total sense. If the message came through an objective third party, not a family member, it had more validity.

SCRATCHING IS SCARY, BUT SAINTLY

Some of you reading this may acknowledge the miraculous circumstances of my sister's death, but also feel that one detail is a bit, well, creepy. After all, the sound of a hand scratching at a window screen frightened my mother and could seem frightening to you as well. You might ask, "Doesn't that sound more scary than saintly?"

Well, I understand that. But consider this: Everything happens for a reason. God is always working in mysterious ways, and I've discovered some things that have helped me see deeper meaning and the hand of God behind those scratching sounds.

As I mentioned in an earlier chapter, my mother was miraculously healed of a goiter after praying to the Infant Jesus of Prague. My sister had formed some close connections with the Sisters of St. Joseph, and through them, cultivated a devotion to St. Therese of Lisieux, who is also known as St. Therese of the Child Jesus. St. Therese herself died young, after suffering immensely from tuberculosis. To her postulants, St. Therese used to say, "I always want to see you behaving like a brave soldier who does not complain about his own suffering, but takes his comrades' wounds seriously and treats his own as nothing but *scratches*." In addition, several months before her death, St. Therese scratched graffiti on the door of her convent cell. She wrote, "JESUS EST MON UNIQUE AMOUR"—*Jesus is my only love*. In her last moments, she was desperate to express the cry of her heart. She wanted to tell the world what she valued most, even as she suffered unbearably.

I think of what Archbishop Gannon said: "I believe your sister is a saint." I agree with him. My sister had absolutely no fear of her own death. She told my mom that she wasn't afraid to die and looked with anticipation to be with God. She considered death to be an adventure and this belief came from her roots in spirituality, which I respected but was incomprehensible to me at that time.

MY SISTER KNEW WE WOULD STRUGGLE

The truth is, maybe my sister knew that, after experiencing her death, me and my family would struggle with making Jesus our only love. And maybe that's why she, like St. Therese, scratched—as a sign for us, something for us to remind us of her faith, her unwavering belief in the love of God.

She was right to leave us with that message. In 1966, the culture was such that one did not speak of death openly and my parents came from a cultural background which did not talk about feelings; thus, they were not inclined to talk openly about what had happened. During this period of my life I was confused and harbored guilt for not saying goodbye to my sister at the hospital. It did not make sense to me that a God who loves me would not allow my beloved sister to live. After her passing, my parents became hurt and mad at God for not stopping my sister's death. They stopped praying and going to Mass.

Thankfully, this only lasted for about three months and with the help and assistance of the Monsignor, they returned to praying and going to Mass. As time passed, God gave the grace that enabled my parents and me to survive the trauma of my sister's death. In addition to the saintly testimony of my sister's life, what helped me was reflecting on Jesus' farewell discourse in the Gospel of John. Jesus gives his followers hope that there is a real relationship, a real presence despite physical absence or distance. He says, "On that day you will know that I am in the Father, and you in me, and I in you" (John 14:20). These words have been of profound comfort and guidance for me as I continue to live into the truth that my sister matters to God and to me, and that I matter to God and to my sister. The relationship has not ended even though my sister died.

When we face a tragedy, or life storms of any kind, it can be extremely difficult. But in the midst of heartache and pain, you can find the hope and courage to go on with God's help as we did. As difficult as this life event was, we realized that we weren't alone. God was with us. He loves us and cares about what is going on in our life. He heard our cries and saw our pain. Moreover, He understands.

That's what my sister believed. She wanted to live like the brave soldier that St. Therese mentioned. She wanted to consider her sufferings "only scratches." And maybe—just maybe—what my sister was trying to do on June 24, 1966 was to desperately scratch a message on that screen door, one that she wanted us to adopt as the cry of our own hearts: *Jesus is my only love.*

CHAPTER FOUR

Fear of Loss or the Flight of Faith?

[31] He who comes from above is above all; he who is of the earth belongs to the earth, and of the earth he speaks; he who comes from heaven is above all. [32] He bears witness to what he has seen and heard, yet no one receives his testimony; [33] he who receives his testimony sets his seal to this, that God is true. [34] For he whom God has sent utters the words of God, for it is not by measure that he gives the Spirit; [35] the Father loves the Son, and has given all things into his hand. [36] He who believes in the Son has eternal life; he who does not obey the Son shall not see life, but the wrath of God rests upon him.

John 3:31-36 (Revised Standard Version)

We can all be fearful of the unknown. We often worry about the things that haven't happened yet—especially if we suspect we are going to lose something we need or love. Consider this common scenario between two people we'll call "Kathy" and "Dave."

> *Kathy comes home from work upset. She doesn't particularly care for her job, but she needs it—and she is concerned that she is in danger of losing it. There are rumors of cut-backs and she is convinced that she would be one of the first to be let go. Her anxiety is exacerbated by the fact that she and her husband, Dave, have just closed on a new home. Can they afford the mortgage if they don't have her income? Absolutely not.*
>
> *Kathy shares her concern with Dave, who listens to her intently and patiently. He lets her express her fears and doubts. Then he hugs her and offers words of encouragement.*
>
> *"If they do let you go," he says, "it will be their loss! But I'm convinced of this," he says. "If you lose that job, it's because God wants you to have a better one!"*

Both Kathy and Dave faced the possibility of loss—in this case, the loss of a job, and thus income and security. In response, Kathy experienced fear. But Dave expressed faith.

How do you respond to the possibility—and even the experience—of loss? Does it worry or frighten you beyond belief? Or do you choose to believe that, regardless of how painful it may be, God has a purpose for it? Simply put: Do you believe God is trustworthy, and that everything will turn out okay in the end?

THE AFTERMATH OF MY SISTER'S PASSING

The traumatic passing of my sister impacted my life and my parents—and we responded in different ways. It seemed to me that my mom and dad became distant from each other. My mom returned to work at GE to help pay for the enormous medical bills incurred for my sister's treatment and my dad buried himself in his business.

I myself became withdrawn for a time; but at the encouragement of my dad, I got more involved in sports. Sometimes getting involved in athletics can be a healthy diversion from life's difficulties, but in this case, it led to forming friendships with people who were not a good influence on me. They had very little morals and seemed to want to party all the time. Suffice it to say, my faith at this time was not very strong.

Time moved on, though, and before I knew it, I was starting college and looking forward to a new beginning. At this time of my life, I was hopeful. I felt that college would help me to mature, relax, and focus more on my education and future.

In the early days of college at Gannon University,

things seemed to be going quite well. Then one day, I was completely broadsided. My girlfriend of only three months shared some shocking news with me: She was pregnant. As she spoke, her words hit my heart and reverberated through my whole body. I confess that, without thinking about it, my initial hope was that she'd get an abortion. But I quickly came to my senses and together we dismissed that option.

Of course, I wasn't the only one who was shocked. So were my parents—although they expressed that shock in different ways. I didn't know how I was going to tell my dad. I was frightened by how he might react. When we finally met with him, he seemed almost struck dumb by the news.

"Take a deep breath before you truly deal with your situation," he said.

Then he added, "Good luck." And walked away.

My mother was less stoic. She was devastated and cried a lot.

My dad remained even-keel. "So what are you going to do?" he asked.

I told him I was going to continue my studies at Gannon.

"How are you going to support the child and the mother?" he asked. "You need to get a full-time job immediately, one with health insurance."

He then went on to suggest that I work third shift at his business, which would enable me to attend college during the day. That sounded good to me. But he wasn't done talking.

"You need to take responsibility," he said. "And do the right thing."

Three weeks later, I married my girlfriend in a wedding ceremony at St. Paul's Catholic Church.

In a way, I guess you could say that my response to the loss of my sister was gaining responsibilities and a life I never planned for.

FIVE YEARS OF FLIGHTS AND FIGHTS

For the next five years I concentrated on my schooling and supporting my family. After graduating in 1973, I immediately started building up my flying hours. A good paying aviation pilot job requires acquiring flight time. So I started flying as much as I could to accumulate flying time.

A private pilot's license is sufficient qualification for flying a small plane, but it won't get you a job as a pilot. Before you can get work flying a 747, DC-10 or other large aircraft, you have to complete the training to earn a commercial pilot's license from the FAA. Some flying jobs require advanced licenses or special certifications as well. I had earned my commercial pilot's license and was looking to build up flying time.

MR. SMITH GOES TO ERIE

One of the main ways I built up my flying time was taking jobs for my dad and his aviation business. On one summer day my dad asked me if I wanted to fly to Detroit City for a pick-up.

"Sure," I said.

Before I left, my dad gave me some advice regarding my flight to Detroit.

"Since you're flying a single-engine aircraft, your flight route should be along the perimeter of the lake," he said. "Not over the lake."

He explained that his reason was safety. In case I experienced an engine failure over the lake, I might not have enough altitude to glide to the shoreline. But if I stayed along the perimeter of the lakeshore, I would be able to pick out a suitable landing area.

I thanked my dad for the advice and took off for Detroit City Airport. The flight only took me about 55 minutes and when I arrived at the Fixed Base Operation at Detroit City Airport, I was greeted by a gentleman who asked me if I was from Erie.

"Yes," I said.

"Great," he answered. "Could you help me load Mr. Smith into the airplane?"

"Sure," I said.

But when I went around the airplane, I saw a hearse and stopped in my tracks.

"Who am I taking back to Erie?" I asked.

"Mr. Smith," answered the man, who was evidently the hearse driver. "He was killed in an automobile accident yesterday."

"His family made arrangements to fly him back."

When I went to the back of the hearse, I noticed that Mr. Smith was just on a stretcher with a white sheet over him.

"What do you want me to do?" I asked, confused.

"Pick him up."

"Wait," I said. "You mean pick up the stretcher and place him in the airplane?"

"No," he said. "This is my stretcher. You're just taking Mr. Smith back."

I grimaced.

"I cannot do this," I said.

I left the hearse driver and Mr. Smith and walked back into the Fixed Base Operation to contact my dad.

"I just can't do this," I said. "I can't pick up and handle a corpse!"

My dad was pretty upset. He lectured me for ten minutes as to why I needed to do what I was asked.

After our conversation, I went out and found a lineperson and offered him $10.00 to assist the hearse driver in loading Mr. Smith into the airplane. He agreed. Problem solved! Or so I thought. After Mr. Smith was loaded into the airplane, I did a pre-flight on the airplane and checked to make sure the corpse was secure. I planned to disregard my father's advice about flying along the perimeter of the lake. After all, I wanted to fly the shortest distance between me and Erie, which meant flying over the lake.

I took off and started climbing to my cruising altitude when I realized that due to the increasing cloud coverage, I needed to go higher to remain in visual flight rules (VFR). At around 13,500 feet, I started to hear a strange noise and started an investigation to locate the source. It didn't take me long to find it. As I turned around, I discovered these noises were coming from Mr. Smith—who was moving!

I became terrified and instantly concluded that Mr. Smith was not dead, but alive! I immediately took the aircraft mike and declared an emergency and asked for a lower altitude. I must have been mumbling my words in a high pitch because the Cleveland air traffic controller couldn't understand my request. He kept saying "repeat that request."

I then pitched the airplane downward and started a rapid descent. I disregarded staying clear of the clouds and my airspeed was approaching the "red" line. I refused to look back at Mr. Smith. I just wanted to get on the ground!

It seemed like an eternity, but I finally landed in Erie, taxied up to my dad's business, jumped out of the airplane, and informed the local hearse driver that Mr. Smith was not deceased. He was still alive! He went over to the airplane to check out my claim while I went into the office to explain to my dad what happened.

As I started to explain my "flight from hell," my dad and several other pilots started laughing.

"What so funny?" I asked.

My dad then explained to me that Mr. Smith wasn't alive, and what I heard was the discharge of gasses and movement being caused by flying at the high altitude. When you fly in a non-pressurized aircraft and a higher altitude is achieved, there are less air molecules and air weight. When you combine these factors with pressure changes, it causes these compensatory responses.

This was embarrassing, but funny at the same time. It's a life lesson I never forgot: What you don't know can lead to a whole lot of fear. Instead of remaining calm, it can cause you to "lose it."

ASHES OVER ERIE

Here's another story I'll never forget:

On a beautiful summer Sunday afternoon, I was in the airport office with my dad discussing the upcoming week's work schedule. At that moment, two men walked into the office and requested the rental of a pilot and plane. They introduced themselves as father and son. The father was holding a small cylindrical jar and seemed very sad. The son explained that the jar contained the remains of his mother and her wish was that her remains be dispersed over their household property when she passed.

They were asking to rent a pilot and a plane to honor her dying wish. My dad said we'd be glad to help and told me to take care of their request. I went and retrieved a local road map and asked them to show me their property.

The husband of the deceased woman was a frail, elderly Italian man who spoke very little English. So the son did most of the communicating and located their property on the map for me. I assumed the son was the one who would be accompanying me on this flight, but he informed me that he didn't like to fly and that his dad, the husband of the deceased, would be accompanying me on this mission.

I pulled the aircraft out of the hangar, loaded up the frail man carrying the remains of his wife, and taxied out for takeoff. Once airborne, it took me about fifteen minutes to reach their property. I started circling his property and told him we were flying directly over it.

He looked down but didn't recognize this as his property.

"Sure it is," I said. "There's your barn and your pond."

"No, this isn't it," he said.

I then realized that everything looks a lot different from an airplane and that this was his first time seeing his home and property from the air. In order to convince him that this indeed was his property, I flew back to the thruway and made sure he identified it as the thruway, which he did. I then flew over the access road from the thruway that leads to his house and made sure he recognized the road and surrounding business establishments, which he did. I then arrived at his house once again.

"Trust me," I said. "This is your house and property."
He still didn't recognize it.

I flew around for about fifteen more minutes, pointing out different property structures and landmarks when suddenly he blurted out, "Yes, I recognize this! This is our home!"

"Thank God, he finally recognizes it," I thought to myself.

I started to configure the airplane for slow flight, putting down flaps to slow down and maneuvering to get aligned over the area where he wanted to disperse his wife's ashes. Suddenly, I heard a loud whoosh of air and saw this gentleman attempting to disperse the contents of the cylindrical jar out the opened aircraft window.

Flying at 85 mph, the contents in that jar were coming right back into the cockpit! The gentleman started screaming, "My wife! My wife!" I reached over and closed the window and attempted to cover my mouth and nose so as not to breathe in the remains of his dearly departed. The husband was in shock and crying. There were still some ashes left in the jar, so I took the jar, cracked open the door and put the remaining contents at the bottom of the door which were sucked-out by the air stream going past the door. That was a more effective method.

I felt nauseous and headed back to the airport as quickly as I could. When I arrived at the parking spot,

I jumped out of the airplane and was making a bee-line to the rest room when my dad intercepted me and asked me what happened. I told him and he did not have a pleasant reaction. He explained to me what I did wrong. When he was finished, I told him I was going home and showering for the rest of the day.

LOSING EARTH, GAINING HEAVEN

Like I asked earlier: How do you respond to the possibility—and experience—of loss? As you just read, my sister's death had a profound effect on me and my parents. Certain things resulted that changed our lives forever. When I thought Mr. Smith had come back to life in my cockpit, I almost "lost it" and crashed my plane! And when that elderly Italian man lost the remains of his wife as we flew over his house and property, he was beside himself. Things didn't go like he wanted them to, and it was very traumatic for him.

The truth is, loss is very traumatic. Looking into the future and seeing the unknown, wondering if we're going to lose our jobs, our homes, or our loved ones—it's very frightening to us. But as we face all of these things, our Father wants us to trust him. Even as we face the biggest of all losses: Death, the loss of our own earthly lives.

Dread of death—and really, the dread of any loss whatsoever—should end when we resolve to make heaven our final destination. The flight of faith should be one characterized by confidence and joy, for "we are citizens of heaven, where the Lord Jesus Christ lives. And we are eagerly waiting for him to return as our Savior" (Phil. 3:20).

CHAPTER FIVE

A Hard Road— And Home Again

When Jesus had spoken these words, he lifted up his eyes to heaven and said, "Father, the hour has come; glorify thy Son that the Son may glorify thee,[2] since thou hast given him power over all flesh, to give eternal life to all whom thou hast given him. [3] And this is eternal life, that they know thee the only true God, and Jesus Christ whom thou hast sent. [4] I glorified thee on earth, having accomplished the work which thou gavest me to do; [5] and now, Father, glorify thou me in thy own presence with the glory which I had with thee before the world was made.

[6] "I have manifested thy name to the men whom thou gavest me out of the world; thine they were, and thou gavest them to me, and they have kept thy word. [7] Now they know that everything that

thou hast given me is from thee; *[8]* for I have given
them the words which thou gavest me, and they
have received them and know in truth that I came
from thee; and they have believed that thou didst
send me. *[9]* I am praying for them; I am not praying
for the world but for those whom thou hast given
me, for they are thine; *[10]* all mine are thine, and
thine are mine, and I am glorified in them. *[11]* And
now I am no more in the world, but they are in the
world, and I am coming to thee. Holy Father, keep
them in thy name, which thou hast given me, that
they may be one, even as we are one.

John 17:1-11 (Revised Standard Version)

If you read the New Testament, you'll see that some
significant journeys take place. After his baptism by
John, Jesus travels into the wilderness where, isolated
from the rest of civilization, he is tempted by the Devil.
Of course, the central and most important journey is
the one Our Lord took to the Cross. As you read the
events leading up to the Crucifixion, it's obvious that,
spiritually speaking, he begins to move away from the
world around him—even away from his family and disciples—and closer to himself and his Father. Eventually, in that moment when he cries, "My God, my God,
why have you forsaken me?" he even moves away from
God. As he bears our sin, he is utterly alone.

Later, well after he rises from the dead, Jesus appears

to Saul of Tarsus as Saul rides down the Damascus road. Persecuting the Church, Saul was headed in the wrong direction; but the Lord calls him into his service and sets him on a new road. Before Saul begins his new life journey as Paul the Apostle, however, he is also sent out to the middle of nowhere—Arabia—to prepare for his vital ministry. For a time, like Jesus, the greatest missionary of the Church must be separated from the rest of the world. He must be alone.

Every time you and I go to Mass, we take a journey. We begin in community. We sit next to each other and together confess our sins, recite the Creed, and listen to the Scripture readings. Eventually, however, we stand up and walk toward the front of the sanctuary. Although we are still among the faithful, in another sense we are by ourselves. Yes, the Eucharist unites us; but when we actually partake of the body, blood, soul, and divinity of Jesus, we experience that moment as individuals. As we remember the suffering of Jesus on our behalf, we are alone.

Yes, the life of faith is a journey that is full of journeys. Like the lives of Jesus and Paul and our experience at Mass, our own spiritual journey may involve walking through the world alone and taking steps that involve suffering. But also like the Lord's life, the Apostle's calling, and the Liturgy, what seems like a journey of isolation and exile is actually the road home. It is the path back to ourselves—and, most important, to God.

A HARD ROAD, A LIFE IN EXILE

From the mid-1970s to the late 1980s, my own journey seemed like an exile. I was walking a hard road of life. I felt as if my soul had moved away from my body. As I walked in this world, I became mired in moral dilemmas and experienced a crisis of faith. I felt as if life had lost its meaning and hope had died—and I wasn't alone. While my parents did not conduct themselves as I did, we all struggled to understand God's will as it related to my sister's death. It was extremely difficult to reconcile Divine Providence and our deep pain in a way that made sense to us. So this was one of the worst times for our family.

A FAMILY CRUSHED

We all felt like we were already in our graves and the earth was piling up on top of us. I buried myself in my studies and worked hard to earn a livable wage for my instant family. I would work the third shift at my father's business, from 11:00 at night until 7:00 in the morning. After that, I'd attend my college classes from 8:30 a.m. to 3:00 p.m. Once I got home, I'd spend the evening plowing through my homework, fall into bed exhausted, and then start the same routine again six hours later. Since I was so busy, my wife depended on her mother to stay with us on the weekdays to help her with our twin boys. Suffice it to say, we had no social or spiritual life for the next five years.

Meanwhile, my dad was being crushed by some huge medical expenses incurred from my sister's kidney treatments. Their financial situation became so dire that thirty years after she retired, my mother had to return to work at General Electric. In addition, my poor dad had a lawsuit filed against all his personal assets by the hospital and several physicians. My mother was convinced that the medical staff had botched my sister's care and was adamant that they were not paying one cent on those bills. She even wanted my dad to take legal action against the hospital and physicians. However, based on legal advice he sought on his own, and without my mother's knowledge, my dad agreed to a financial settlement that ended the lawsuit. Several months later, my mother found out about the settlement and was furious. This caused an even wider rift between them.

BACK TO MASS

After eight months, our parish pastor, Father James Daley, visited my mom and dad and had a heart-to-heart discussion with them. They talked about my sister's passing and our disengagement from the Church community. He said he understood our pain and let us know that when we were ready, he would like to see us rejoin the faith community at Our Lady of Peace. He was gentle and sensitive. About two months later, we began attending regular Sunday Mass again.

A LESSON IN LEADERSHIP

Once I graduated, I expected life to go a little easier. I approached my dad about a job opening at his business.

"I'm ready for that open management position," I said.

"I beg your pardon?" he said.

"Well, I have a degree now," I said. "I'm ready for that management position."

He opened up his desk drawer and handed me an application.

"Fill this out and I'll take a look at it," he said.

I was incredulous.

"Is this a joke?" I asked.

"Absolutely not," he said. "If you want another position, fill out the application."

I just shook my head. But I filled it out and returned it to my dad. About three days later, he called me into his office and informed me that there was an opening on second shift on the line crew.

"What?" I exclaimed. "The line crew?"

"Yes," he said calmly.

The line crew job was basically hard labor. It involved refueling aircraft, cleaning, storage, and a few other tasks I deemed menial. I told him I had a college degree and that I deserved better. He responded by saying that if I wanted to move up in the company, I would need to start at the bottom and work my way up like everyone else.

"Don't like it?" he said. "Go somewhere else."

That exchange sure deflated my ego. But after a short minute's thought, I accepted the position. I worked my rear-end off for six months, and after six-months my dad promoted me to line-supervisor. I was in charge of all three shifts, including hiring and firing of personnel. I jumped in with both feet. I developed the company's first line-crew manual, which set up procedures and created job descriptions. In my mind, I was utilizing my college education to make a difference for my dad's company. I called a mandatory employee meeting for all three shifts and handed out my line-crew manual and spent two hours going over the manual and new job descriptions. I was feeling pretty good and enjoyed the feeling of power. But after I was finished with my presentation and asked for questions, one of the employees blurted out, "Are you serious?"

"I sure am," I said.

Protests erupted from the group.

"This is ridiculous," one employee said.

"You're an ass," added another.

Except for one man, they all quit on the spot and walked out.

I was dumbfounded. I didn't know what to do. I ran to the phone and called my dad to explain what had just occurred.

"Well, son, guess you have a big problem on your hands," he said calmly. "Good luck." Then he hung-up.

For the next three months, I had to work two shifts by myself until I hired a work force to replace the walk-outs. It was hard, but I got through it and learned the valuable lesson that my dad wanted me to learn. I never would have learned it if he had started me in a management position. And the lesson is this: Workers are human beings who need to be treated, as the Gospel says, with love and dignity. I never forgot that lesson.

THINGS LOOK UP, THEN GO DOWN

Four years later, in 1979, I was moving along in life nicely, confident that I would achieve my goals. My dad was preparing me to take over his business one day. I was finally becoming debt free, starting to build up my emergency fund, and getting ready to actively invest and save for retirement. Everything seemed to be going great; but then life started knocking me down again.

First, my uncle Joe, my dad's brother and the vice president of the business, was diagnosed with colon cancer. Then the second oil crisis, or "oil shock" as they called it, occurred in the United States due to decreased oil output. Those turn of events rocked our business.

My dad and his two brothers were in their sixties. When the oil crisis hit, my dad, without telling anyone (including my mom), started actively looking for someone to buy his company. In the summer of 1979, my dad was approached by a local individual who owned an insurance company and wanted to make an offer on my dad's business. My dad was open to the offer, but requested that one condition of the sales agreement would be keeping me on as president of the company.

The buyer rejected this condition. He wanted his own accountant, who had zero experience or skills in the aviation business, to become the new president. In spite of this, my dad and his brothers agreed to the offer and in September of 1979 my dad informed me that he sold the business. I was devastated. I couldn't believe it.

"Why did you do this?" I asked him.

"It was time to retire," he said.

For the next three month, my dad stayed and helped the new owners get acquainted with the employees and business procedures. I was moved to Director of Commuter Operations and also served as a fill-in charter pilot. As I said, the new president had no clue about the business or aviation, but I cooperated with him as much as he would let me. But after two-and-a-half years of working with the new owners, Tom Daggett, the president, called me into his office and informed me that my position was being eliminated.

"Okay," I said. "I'll just go back to line flying."

"No," he responded. "There is no position here for you."

I told him that I had fifteen years of seniority, which should make me eligible to re-position within the company.

"We pay for performance," he responded. "Not seniority."

"What does that mean?" I asked.

"It means you no longer have a job with this company," he said.

I went into shock. I walked out of his office like a zombie and drove immediately to my dad's house to explain what just happened. He was very upset and told me he would make some calls the next day. His calls to the owner resulted in nothing more than a "Sorry, there is nothing I can do" response from the owner. I didn't know what to do. I envisioned being at my dad's business until I retired. I started to become anxious, scared, and depressed.

My wife didn't seem to recognize how traumatic this life-changing event was for me and just wanted me to look for another job as soon as possible. But the country was basically in a recession and there were no job openings locally. So, I decided to start my own business, Erie County Flying Service. It was a business in which I offered my pilot and aviation services to anyone who needed them in the tri-state area. It was tough sledding for the next couple of years. I had to register for food stamps and applied for every government assistance program I was eligible for. Those programs helped me keep my head above water during that period of my life.

DEALT ANOTHER BLOW

Then in November of 1982, another bomb exploded. I learned that my dad, like his brother, was also diagnosed with colon cancer. Medicine can often treat a condition, but it doesn't guarantee that full healing will take place. Surgery may sometimes be necessary for healing, but it is never sufficient. This is because total healing involves, not just our bodies, but also our minds and spirits. That's something standard medicine can't touch. With this in mind, I turned to God for the healing of my dad. I was saying Novenas, going to daily Mass, sometimes walking eight miles to church, hoping for a cure for my dad.

Several weeks after my dad's diagnosis, the doctors performed the operation to remove the tumor, but were unsuccessful in removing all of it. Ultimately, they had to remove three quarters of his colon; in doing so, they made it necessary for my dad to undergo a colostomy and begin weekly radiation treatments.

My dad was a fighter and he fought his disease with all his strength. But after about a month, my dad developed a very bad headache. The hospital ran some tests and discovered that his colon tumor had spread to his brain. Against the doctors' wishes, my mom adamantly insisted that my dad not be told about the brain tumor. The news would be demoralizing.

Several days later, when we were in my dad's hospital room, the nurse arrived and started to prepare my dad for the radiation treatments on his head. The nurse was getting him ready when he asked her, "Where are we going?"

"We're taking you down for radiation on your head," she said.

"My head!" he said. "I just have a headache. I don't need radiation on my head!"

The nurse realized what was happening and called for a doctor. When the doctor arrived, he explained to my dad that his tumor had spread to his brain and that we needed to start treating that area immediately with radiation.

I looked at my dad and waited for his response. But he just hung his head down and said nothing. I knew right then and there that he had given up. He probably wondered why no one told him about this new development.

DAD LEAVES THE LIGHT ON

On May 5, 1983, at 2:30 in the afternoon, my dad passed into eternity. He was surrounded by his family, everyone except for my mother. At the time, I just assumed that it was too difficult for her. My sister had died just over ten years prior and my mother was still dealing with that loss. She just couldn't bear to watch my dad pass, too. But a half hour after his final breath, she arrived at the hospital, to be with her husband.

Since my mother was grieving and in no condition to organize anything, I was put in charge of making arrangements for my dad's funeral, the funeral Mass, and the wake. After the funeral Mass, we invited everyone to my mom and dad's home for the wake. When we walked into the house, the first thing I noticed was the living room wall clock had mysteriously dislodged from the wall mounting and fallen to the floor. My jaw dropped. The clock had stopped running at the exact time my dad passed.

During the wake, my best friend Harry approached me and asked me where the light switch was for the patio. I told him that it was right behind him. He immediately turned around, looked at the switch, and then walked over and just stared at it. Harry, an electrician, just couldn't take his eyes off the light switch.

His actions caught my attention.

"Why are you so fascinated with this light switch?" I asked.

He turned, looked at me with a very serious expression, and said, "I've never seen this before!"

"Are you serious?" I asked. "What do you mean?"

He then began to explain to me that the light in the patio was continuing to cycle on and off without anyone touching the light switch.

"I'm telling you," he said again. "I have never seen this before."

The group of people in the patio were reminiscing about my dad. They were unaware of the light over the table cycling on and off. I was astonished at this phenomenon and blurted out, "Hey everyone! Look at the light over the table!"

It became very quiet and the light flashed several more times, then stopped. My aunt Sophie immediately started praying the Hail Mary and then everyone else joined her. That afternoon, we all had a calming sense of my dad's presence.

Several months later, I went to Mass, and afterward, a priest gave a talk about Fatima, Portugal.

"If anyone is interested in going on this trip to Fatima," he said. "They need to register within two weeks."

FATIMA AND A FAILED MARRIAGE

I was excited and interested in the opportunity. I rushed home to discuss it with my wife. She wasn't very enthused, but finally, after much pleading, agreed to go. Unfortunately, she used the trip as nothing more than a vacation and opportunity to shop. But for me, the trip was a spiritual shot in the arm. It ministered to my soul and helped me start to get back to my old self again.

I was the executor of my dad's estate and was honoring his wishes in the will. The bulk of his estate naturally went to my mother. However, my dad left me some annuities and his 1959 MGA. My wife was disappointed that I didn't receive more money from his will. She told me that I better get out and start looking for a decent job. I wasn't worried; between unemployment compensation and my flying business, we were doing okay—at least financially.

Our relationship was another story. Over the next several months, I definitely noticed a change in my wife's behavior and attitude. I was so concerned that I met with her dad and asked for his input and advice. He told me not to worry.

"I know my daughter and everything is just fine," he said.

But that wasn't the truth—not even close. Several days later, my wife served me with divorce papers. In addition, I discovered that she had withdrawn half of our joint checking account, including proceeds from my dad's annuity.

In spite of this, I didn't want to give up. I sat down with my wife and discussed my desire to make the marriage work. After I finished, she told me that she was finished and was not open to marriage counseling or talking to a priest.

"I just want out," she said.

I pleaded with her to reconsider. She said "no" and told me that I needed to move on with my life. "I'm moving on with mine," she said.

Once I realized there was no convincing her to reconsider her decision, I asked her about her future plans and the plans she had for our twin boys.

"I'll never get married again," she said. "I'm going to be a successful person."

She then told me we needed to sell the house and divide the proceeds.

"Someday," I said. "I will remarry, God willing. And I will find a good job with great pay."

I remember this very clearly: She just laughed at me.

"Who in the world would want to marry you?" she asked. "You're a loser."

That remark cut to my soul. We had been married for fifteen years and I suddenly felt as if I never knew her. Yes, over the course of our marriage, I wasn't the best husband or father. I wasn't there in the beginning to help with the boys; but that was, in large part, because I was studying so hard and working long hours to provide for my family—both in the present and in the future.

A MESSY AFTERMATH

Unfortunately, it was a messy divorce and our boys were caught in the middle. My wife was focused on making sure that my child support payments were on time, but was not focused on making sure the boys received their high school education. Even though I had visiting rights, my wife made sure that they were not available when it was time for me to see them. They never received all the personal letters that I sent to them. She made sure of that.

A couple more years passed, and even though my boys were almost twenty years old, they hadn't graduated high school. In fact, they had even stopped going to school altogether—and my now ex-wife was not making any effort to change that scenario.

I finally requested a child support hearing and pointed this all out to the judge. He chastised my wife for her behavior and two months later terminated my child support payments.

While all this was going on, there was even more family conflict. My mother filed a law-suit against my ex-father-in-law for repayment of my dad's investment in his car lot. This was because my mom discovered from a number of sources that about a week before my dad passed, my ex-wife and her dad approached my dad in his hospital room and had him sign a disillusionment form from his business. Ultimately, my mom's lawyer counseled her that she could contest the signing, but that my ex-father-in-law had no real assets and that pursuing litigation would be fruitless. She agreed.

SAVED BY ROSES

I felt like my life was reeling out of control. All the stress had affected me physically, emotionally, and spiritually. I stopped eating, withdrew socially, and stopped going to Mass. My emotions got the best of me. It wasn't uncommon for me to shout obscenities when things went wrong. I couldn't get happy about anything. I quit caring about my appearance. I did not want to admit that I couldn't handle things the way they were.

Finally, I decided that I needed to get away. I called Harry and told him I was leaving and not to worry. I got into my car and started driving. Within a half hour, I entered Ohio. It was night time and raining hard. I saw a hotel and stopped to see if they had a room available for one night. They did.

Once inside, I started drinking. After several hours of drinking, I remembered that I had a full bottle of prescription drugs in my suitcase. The pills were pain relievers. I started to take a pill every half hour and became more and more tired. The combination of the alcohol and pills produced a numbing, drowsy feeling and made me forget about all my worries. Then, for reasons I don't understand but certainly under the influence of those substances, I suddenly grabbed the bottle of prescription drugs and gulped down the remaining pills.

That was an act of desperation and despair, and I was clearly not in my right mind. But somehow, in the midst of that physical and emotional fog, the Holy Spirit prompted an act of faith. I began to pray to St. Therese the Little Flower by saying the Rosary—and I suddenly felt a sense of peace.

The next thing I knew, it was morning. I sat up, took a deep breath, and immediately smelled the fragrance of roses. I went to the door, opened it, and looked down.

Lying on the doorstep was a single rose.

I looked out toward the highway and noticed the hotel sign. I hadn't noticed the name before. It read:

"The Rose Garden Inn."

Talk about a sign! If that wasn't one, I didn't know what was.

I found a phone booth and called Harry. He was thrilled to hear my voice and said that I needed to call my uncle Andy right away. I hung up and called him.

"Are you all right?" he asked.

"I am now," I said.

"Look, Dennis," he said. "I know things have been tough for you over the last year or so, but that's all in the past. You can't change it. You need to look forward and concentrate on the future."

"There are a lot of people who love you," he added. "Me, your mother, your sons, aunts, and uncles—and all of us want the best for you."

His words meant a lot to me. And I was still overwhelmed with gratitude for the gift of the roses—sent, I was sure, by St. Therese.

"You're right, Uncle Andy," I said. "I'm coming home."

HARD ROADS CAN LEAD HOME, TOO

What about you? Have you walked some hard roads in life? Have you felt—maybe you still feel—as if your soul has left your body, that you are in exile from your own life? As you have read, I've been there.

Never in a million years would I ever minimize the suffering I've experienced or the bad choices I often made in response to pain. But I will tell you——in all honesty and sincerity—that, looking back, there was never a time when there wasn't some indication of God's presence through it all. It might have been a much-needed trip to Fatima to re-energize my faith, a flickering light in the living room, or the gift of a single rose.

I fully believe that there is meaning in everything we experience—even those events that break our hearts. I also believe that the people who achieve real peace and joy in this earthly journey learn to accept life on its own terms. They adjust to it as it presents itself instead of allowing themselves to be crushed by its seemingly cruel indifference.

Ultimately, a person's capacity to have faith in troubled times differentiates those who overcome from those who are overwhelmed. The willingness to relinquish control and leave ego behind when there seems to be little other choice is what separates the saintly from the insane.

Listen to me: If you have walked a hard road, I understand. Believe me: It's no good to let life's hardships harden *you*. Trust me: Even though you may not feel it at times, God is—and always has been—walking that road with you. At any time, you can turn to him—and come home.

CHAPTER SIX

Unexpected Graces...
And What God Expects of Us

Watch therefore, for you do not know on what day your Lord is coming. ⁴³ But know this, that if the householder had known in what part of the night the thief was coming, he would have watched and would not have let his house be broken into.⁴⁴ Therefore you also must be ready; for the Son of man is coming at an hour you do not expect.

⁴⁵ "Who then is the faithful and wise servant, whom his master has set over his household, to give them their food at the proper time? ⁴⁶ Blessed is that servant whom his master when he comes will find so doing. ⁴⁷ Truly, I say to you, he will set him over all his possessions. ⁴⁸ But if that wicked servant says to himself, 'My master is delayed,' ⁴⁹ and begins to beat his fellow servants, and eats and drinks with

> *the drunken, [50] the master of that servant will come*
> *on a day when he does not expect him and at an*
> *hour he does not know, [51] and will punish[a] him,*
> *and put him with the hypocrites; there men will*
> *weep and gnash their teeth*

Matthew 24:42-51

Several years ago, a friend of mine served at a retreat program held at a local prison. The program was hosted for the small group of inmates who were willing to participate. For three days, my friend would minister to these men, and during that time, they would tell him stories that he would later tell me. Even though some of the offenses the men committed were very serious, they continued to regard them with a sense of humor. Admittedly, the stories were often very funny.

One inmate—we'll call him James—recounted the time he exchanged words with an exasperated judge. As he delivered the sentencing, the judge cried, "James, you have to STOP breaking the law!"

"But judge," James replied. "I'm a criminal. It's what I do!"

Judas Iscariot was a criminal. The Bible refers to him as a thief; and I often wonder if Jesus was prompted to compose a thievery-themed parable because of his association with, and deep knowledge of, the man who would someday betray him. Whether that was a factor or not, the point of the parable is clear: When the

Son of Man comes, it will be like a thief—a thief in the night.

A thief doesn't announce his coming. In fact, his whole intention is to get in, do his "business," and get out—completely undetected. In a similar way, when God acts, he does it when we are not expecting it. This principle holds true, not only for the return of Jesus Christ, but for the way God often deals with us throughout our whole lives.

I believe that, day by day, God's grace comes to us in a lot of different guises and we often miss it. We need to understand that our opportunities to respond to God's invitations are limited.

God has given all of us time, talent, and treasure. Every day, he puts these gifts at our disposal, to be used to build up the Kingdom of God. God's presence is upon us, in us, and with us, so that we can make him present to the whole world. Do we?

The wizard Gandalf is a character from *The Lord of the Rings*, written by that great Catholic author J.R.R. Tolkien. Gandalf is very wise, and in one passage of the novel he says, "All we have to decide is what to do with the time that is given us."

What do we do with our time? How do we use it to exercise our talents and invest our treasure? Considering all that God has given us, how would you and I fare if we had to give an accounting *today*?

A NEW START

After talking with my uncle Andy, I returned home and attempted to start my life over again, recalling the words of G.K. Chesterton: "Think of all those ages through which men have had the courage to die, and then remember that we have actually fallen to talking about having the courage to live." With this in mind, I decided to honestly face up to my situation and determine what the most valuable things in life really are. Once I was firmly resolved, it didn't take me long to discover what I already knew. The most valuable things in my life were my faith, my children, my family, and my friends. Earlier in my life, I probably would have said I valued these things. But we human beings often claim something is vitally important to us, then fail to invest the kind of time and attention that would back up that claim. I was like that. In some ways, we all are.

My friend Harry offered me a small office area that I could use for my flying service business. I was excited—and a bit desperate. I accepted any and all offers of work, which included washing the outside and cleaning the inside of various aircraft. There were many twelve hour days, which gave me little time to look for other employment. After several months of being an entrepreneur, I was approached by a pilot friend of mine who asked me if I would be interested in flying for a commuter airline. There were several local investors who decided to start a regional commuter airline service for the Erie community, and they were looking for pilots.

When you've been out of paid work for a number of months, or even a few years, and you want to return to work, it becomes hard to know what to expect. At least that is my experience. Your industry or workplace may have gone through some changes. The position and skills associated with the job may also have changed. Knowing that, I still jumped at the prospect and submitted my application. Within twenty-four hours, I received a call for an interview. It was a very short interview and when the human relations person finished, he informed me that I was hired. I accepted the job immediately.

"Ground School starts in two hours in the maintenance room," he said.

"Ground School" was basically a crash course on the BA-3100 and it was essentially left up to each person to learn the airplane. After two weeks, I began flight training; and after a month, I passed my flight test and was an official commuter airline pilot.

I thought putting in 12 hour days in my own business was hard! It didn't compare to the working hours and flight time that I was putting in for this start-up airline. I basically had no free time. After all, I worked six days a week, and each day was very, very long. The good news was that I was home every night. That was important to me because I was able to help my mother if she needed me.

This situation continued for about six months until the company selected me for an upgrade to Captain. Not only did I accomplish the upgrade, but I also became the company's instructor for other pilots upgrading to Captain. That was more of a time commitment, but I accepted that position because I thought it would look good on my resumé.

PERIL AS A PILOT INSTRUCTOR

One time I was giving instruction at night to a pilot who was upgrading to Captain. That night's schedule had me going over V1 cuts. That is when an airplane reaches "decision" speed, the speed at which you either take off or terminate the flight. This pilot was doing a pretty good job and, as we took off, I relaxed a little—which is something you never want to do in that situation. As part of a training exercise, I cut off the power to one engine. Still too relaxed, I was not quick enough to prevent him from recognizing the wrong engine. He froze at the controls, rendering me helpless.

"Let go of the controls!" I yelled.

He didn't respond.

I tried to override the controls, but was unable to do so, and we were descending quickly. The ground was coming up fast!

"I have the aircraft," I told him. "Let go!"

Still no response.

Finally, I did the only thing I could think of: I punched

81

him in the face. Immediately, he let go of the controls. I took over and regained control of the aircraft. The plane landed safely.

We taxied up to the ramp with no one saying a word. I shut down the airplane

"What happened to you up there?" I asked.

"I don't know," he said. "I have never done that before."

I discussed with him what had happened, what he should have done, and he understood.

"I'm ready to go up again," he said.

I looked at him.

"Come with me," I said.

We left the airport. I took him over to a local bar and grille.

"Today's lesson is over," I said.

The next day I went to Mass. I thanked God for saving us from what could have been a very bad accident. I then went to the Chief Pilot's office and resigned as a pilot instructor.

ANNULMENT AND A NEW LOVE

Since my divorce was finalized, I had many well-intentioned friends "arranging" dates for me. But it was over a decade since I dated and I felt very uncomfortable. As I thought about navigating the scary world of dating again, a question entered my mind: If I wanted to marry again, would I need to receive an annulment from the Catholic Church?

The church's process for declaring a marriage null was a mystery to me. I think that the Church's tribunal proceedings are mysterious to many people, because they date back to ancient times, are originally written in Latin, and are concerned with complex matters of theology and procedural law. I was confused over annulments because of the Church's teaching on the indissolubility of marriage and its annulment procedures, which are seemingly contradictory. However, as I found out, these two realities are not in opposition, but rather balance one another. For when the Church teaches what marriage is, it is also teaching what marriage is not. A declaration of nullity is not a dissolution of marriage; it is not a Church divorce. Rather, it is a judicial finding that a marriage had not been brought about on the wedding day, as the faith community had presumed. Admittedly, I was somewhat concerned about my former wife's response to my petition and her false contentions about my character as a husband and father during our marriage. However, the tribunal investigated my petition for about nine months and, by God's grace, they concluded that the conditions were not met for marriage. I was granted my annulment.

Not long after, one of my friends introduced me to the receptionist at the local Fixed Base Operation that I was flying out of. Her name was Lynn and right from the beginning, we hit it off. She was also recently divorced and had a baby girl from her previous marriage. Over the next three years, we developed a very close relationship and found that we had a lot in common. I was attending Mass on a regular basis and Lynn and her daughter joined me. It seemed like my life was back on track, that it was good again.

CONTINENTAL CALLS

Then one day I received a notice from my Chief Pilot that our airline was moving its headquarters out of Erie to Baltimore, Maryland. This would require a move on my part. I was in a quandary on what to do. Lynn was working at a local law office and was in no position to move herself and her daughter to Baltimore. About a week later, however, I received an invitation for a job interview with Continental Airlines in Houston, Texas. That was the job I was working toward ever since I started flying. I wanted to fly for a major airline. I was excited and so was Lynn.

The following week, I traveled down to Houston for the interview. It went well and the Human Relations manager told me I had the job, provided my blood tests results came back satisfactory. I was elated. I returned to Erie and immediately gave my two-week notice to my employer. My Chief Pilot was not very pleased and let me know about it.

Two days before I was to leave my job in Erie, I received a Fed-Ex letter rescinding my offer for employment. The letter stated that my blood tests were not satisfactory. I called Continental to discuss the letter and found out that my blood test showed that I had an elevated level of iron. I thought iron was a good thing, but apparently elevated iron levels make your blood thicker. In turn, your heart has to work harder—which of course creates a safety problem for pilots.

I asked if I could re-take the blood test over because it could have been caused by some cold medication that I was taking. They said "sure" and told me to take the blood test locally and fax the results to them. I agreed. Then I remembered that in two days I would be out of work, so I called my Chief Pilot and told him that I reconsidered and no longer wanted to leave my job. He read me the riot act and told me that he needed that in writing. So I typed up a letter recanting my letter of resignation and hand delivered it to him. He accepted it.

Three days later, I received a call from Continental informing me that my iron levels were within limits, I had to show up for class in two weeks. I was overjoyed. I then typed out my second letter of resignation to my Chief Pilot. Of course, I wasn't looking forward to his reaction—which I was sure was going to involve cursing and gnashing of teeth.

When I arrived in his office, however, something amazing happened. Before I could give him my letter of resignation, he told me that "due to insufficient pilot staffing," he was changing my entire work schedule for that month.

"Are you kidding?" I asked. "I'm the fourth senior pilot in the company. You can't do that!"

"I am doing it," he said. "And if you don't like it, quit"

Talk about Divine Providence!

"I quit," I said.

"I need that in writing," he said.

I put my hand in my pocket, pulled out my letter of resignation, and walked out. I will never forget the look on his face!

NEW COMMITMENTS

I made a commitment to Continental Airlines. In my opinion, in order for us to know how to commit, we need to understand what it means to be committed. Our needs are changing, and we live in a society where our individuality is emphasized as a big part of who we are and our process of growth. Commitment means making something strong and healthy.

I was looking for true love, a soul mate, and I found that in Lynn. So the day after I quit my job in Erie, I proposed to Lynn. She accepted and we set our wedding day for May 7th, 1988. My flight school classes started on February 5th, 1988 and ended May 1st.

On my first day of class, we were told what equipment we would be trained on and where we would be based. I couldn't believe it: I was assigned to the DC-10 and would be based in Honolulu, Hawaii. 5,000 miles away from Lynn!

The one caveat the people at Continental mentioned was that everyone would only be at their base, and on that equipment, for six months. Afterward, we would be awarded our preferred base and aircraft. I wanted to fly the 737 out of Cleveland.

My class was in Los Angeles and, as I mentioned, lasted for twelve weeks. The training was hard and fast-paced. I was only able to return home for one weekend. That meant that Lynn was handling all the arrangements for our wedding. After about a month in training, I started experiencing anxiety, worrying about the prospect of failing the course and being out of a job. I was positive that my previous chief pilot would never re-hire me, and I started thinking I could be an unemployed married man.

At that time, Continental had a high "wash-out" rate for new hires. Before each class, I started attending Mass every day. It was a comfort for me and gave me strength to accept whatever was in store for me in the future. When I reflect on those days, I sense the awe and wonder, the moments of grace that are necessarily part and parcel of the encounter I experienced.

NEAR MISS

The day before I was to take my check ride, my instructor failed me for advancement. I was devastated. I thought my whole career with the airlines was over. I crashed and burned. But then I went to Mass that night and had a sense of peace come over me. The next day I was called into the chief flight instructor's office. He was a very nice man and began to explain to me that the reason he called me in was that a number of my classmates approached him and complained that I was treated unfairly by my ground instructor. They told him the instructor purposely designed the questions to confuse me and have me "wash-out" of the program. He said that he wanted to change that "mentality" in the organization and that he would personally administer my oral and flight exam. He proceeded with the oral exam, which lasted about forty minutes. He said he felt that I knew the systems of the DC-10 sufficiently to proceed with the flight test in the simulator the next day. It was just the two of us who showed up at the simulator at 6:30 in the morning. We proceeded with the flight test; it took an hour and fifteen minutes. When it concluded, he looked at me and smiled.

"You did a fine job," he said. "You are now a Flight Engineer on a DC-10 for Continental Airlines."

FOUR, THREE, TWO...

I was ecstatic. I left for home that very day. It was a five-hour flight and I would arrive with just four days to get ready for our wedding. When I arrived home the next morning, before I could say anything, Lynn told me she had something to tell me. I worried that she had changed her mind and no longer wanted to get married. Instead, she told me that the whole time I was in flight training, she knew how important my faith was and wanted to be at the same "level" as I was. So before we were married, she wanted to receive the sacrament of the Eucharist and the sacrament of Confirmation. (When Jesus spoke of the sacraments, he made clear that they were essential and that the family table forms not only our bodies but also our minds and souls.) My wife's desires were fulfilled. Prior to our marriage, she was confirmed in the Catholic Church and partook of the body, blood, soul, and divinity of our Lord in the Eucharist.

Our wedding day was absolutely beautiful, and even the weather held up when it needed to. I was especially thankful to have my mom alive to participate in our ceremony. Every piece of the ceremony made clear what was important to us, not only that we loved each other, but that our love was rooted in faith. Lynn and I knew the significance of the sacrament that we conferred on one another and were receiving the graces necessary to start our new life together. However, being together had to wait.

HAPPY AT LAST

After our honeymoon, I returned to work, which meant getting up at five in the morning, driving 100 miles to Cleveland, getting on a plane, flying five hours to Los Angeles, switching planes, then flying another five hours to Honolulu and arriving around 12:00 noon, which was 6:00 pm local Erie time. I was on the island for twenty days straight before I could leave to go home. I would lose two days traveling to and from work, so basically I was only home for five days a month.

This wasn't the best way to start a marriage, but we knew it was just temporary and things would get better down the road. Or so we thought. After my six months with the company, I bid for a new base and equipment, as was promised when I was hired. That was not to be. Because of low staffing and equipment problems, I was informed that I would be based in Honolulu indefinitely. After completing my first year with the company, I received a TDY (temporary duty assignment) to Guam. I didn't even know where Guam was, but when I found out, I knew I wouldn't be able to commute home on my days off.

Lynn received the news of my transfer with grace and understanding. She was basically running the household and raising her daughter by herself. Juggling motherhood, doing housework, taking care of three dogs, paying bills, and facing whatever else happened along the way by herself was no easy task. But what kept her focused and grounded during this time was her faith.

There were days when everything was just buoyant and an unexpected equilibrium was reached, and on those days we experienced real happiness.

"How did this happen to me?" I asked myself. "I am truly blessed to be alive."

Of course, happiness comes and goes. But attending Mass on a regular basis gave me a great sense of purpose along with many other joys. St. Paul asks that as Christians we learn to prize the things that are of value. And one of the most basic values of Mass is remembrance. The righteous person lives by faith.

ONE OF THESE LEAST

Here's a quick, but important side story of something that happened during this time of my life: There is no doubt in my mind that the Liturgy leads us through the visible signs of sacraments to the invisible reality of God's grace. But we need to cooperate with that grace. I remember one day, after attending Mass in Honolulu, I was walking back to my apartment. I was on a sidewalk just adjacent from the main thoroughfare and I noticed an individual a good distance from me. He looked very haggard and obviously was homeless. I didn't want to engage this individual, because I didn't want to give him the cash I had in my pocket, which I was going to use for breakfast. So I abruptly walked across the street to the sidewalk and continued my journey. When I looked up, I saw this individual again walking towards me; so I quickly crossed the street again and was startled to see the same individual again, but much closer. As we approached each other, I put my head down and turned up my Walkman so as not to have to respond to any request he might make. I hadn't taken more than three steps after passing this individual when my conscience (The Holy Spirit!) kicked in and told me to engage this individual. I quickly turned around and was reaching into my pocket to give this person some money when I was shocked to see no one. There wasn't anyone in sight on my sidewalk or the sidewalk on the other side of the street. There were just empty fields on both sides of the street and no one around. It was like he just disappeared into thin air.

I resumed my walk and thought about what had just happened. I thought then as I do now that person was Jesus. I ignored him because I didn't want to give up some of my breakfast money. Needless to say, I didn't have breakfast that morning, but I did pay for someone else's breakfast in the restaurant I normally frequented in the mornings. I decided then and there that I would never again turn down a person who needed or asked for assistance. I felt that it isn't up to me to decide who this person is or what he or she is going to do with the money. Anytime I give a person on the street some money, I tell them: "What you do with this is between you and God. But may God Bless you."

CLEARED FOR CLEVELAND

After four years of being at four other bases, I was finally awarded the Cleveland base, flying the Boeing 737. It was great. I could commute to work every week and the one hour and fifty minute drive was nothing compared to the days of flying for ten hours to go to work. In 1993 God blessed our family with the arrival of our daughter, Danielle. What a joy! (I'd like to also mention that in 2001, my step-daughter Krystal Pellican asked me to adopt her. She became Krystal Kudlak. More joy!)

Several years later, I was able to hold Captain for Continental airlines, which is the "pilot-in-command" of an airplane and the position which all pilots strive for in their airline career.

I successfully completed my upgrade training for Captain and accomplished the goal I had worked towards for the past ten years. You would think I would be very happy. I was, but I felt that something was missing and I couldn't put my finger on it. Then one day at Mass I heard about a program that the Diocese had for Catholic men called the Permanent Diaconate. This program required not just the man's commitment, but the acceptance and participation of his wife, if he was married. When I discussed my desire to enroll in the program with Lynn, she wasn't on board. She felt that being just upgraded to Captain, along with the time involved with the Diaconate, wouldn't leave much time for the family. She also felt that I needed to get closer with our recently born daughter. After thinking about it some more, I agreed. I put the thought of becoming a permanent deacon on the back burner.

So that's the way my life unfolded at this time. It was moment after moment of unexpected—but much appreciated—grace. I've learned that God loves giving mercy and grace to us. But the thing is, there were times I was ready for it and times that I wasn't. God is always ready and willing to give us gifts. In fact, he's eager to lavish them on us. The key is that we have to be prepared to receive them.

CHAPTER SEVEN

Be All You Can Be

That's the slogan that was once used by the United States Army.

For me, "be all you can be" meant achieving my primary goal in life, which was to become a Captain at a major airline. I thought that once I achieved this goal, my life would be very satisfying. I would have a great feeling of accomplishment, both personally and professionally.

But then I read Mark 8:27-35:

Jesus and his disciples set out
For the villages of Caesarea Philippi.
Along the way he asked his disciples,
"Who do people say that I am?"
They said in reply,
"John the Baptist, others Elijah,

Still others one of the prophets."
And he asked them,
"But who do you say that I am?"
Peter said to him in reply,
"You are the Christ."
Then he warned them not to tell anyone about him.
He began to teach them
That the Son of Man must suffer greatly
And be rejected by the elders, the chief priests, and the scribes,
And be killed, and rise after three days.
He spoke this openly.
Then Peter took him aside and began to rebuke him.
At this he turned around and, looking at his disciples,
Rebuked Peter and said, "Get behind me, Satan.
You are thinking not as God does, but as human beings do."
He summoned the crowd with his disciples and said to them,
"Whoever wishes to come after me must deny himself,
Take up his cross, and follow me.
For whoever wishes to save his life will lose it,
But whoever loses his life for my sake
And that of the gospel will save it."

After I read that, I knew that God had much more in store for me.

COMMON SAYINGS AT COMMENCEMENTS

Have you ever heard these sayings?

- "Do what you love and love what you do."

- "Follow your passions."

- "Do what you love and you'll never work a day in your life."

I suppose that every high school and college graduate, or anyone in the first steps of making their way in life, has heard those sayings. The "do what you love" philosophy has been around for quite some time, but it gained even more momentum when it was espoused in a commencement address by Steve Jobs, the late, great technology innovator and CEO of Apple. He delivered that message not once, but several times. He said, "Your life, hopefully, will be filled largely with great work—you want to do great work—but in order to do great work, you have to love what you do."

Given the passage in Mark that I quoted above, straight from the mouth of Christ, who is the very personification of wisdom, what should we say about Jobs' philosophy of "do what you love"?

Without taking away from his accomplishments, consider this: A lot of people worked under Jobs holding positions that I'm fairly certain they did not love. The goods of his company were assembled and packaged in those real nice, stunning white and silver cases—and I doubt that people particularly delighted in the task. (I still remember years and years ago when the first iPod came out. I was sitting around "ooing and awing" about the packaging as I was opening it up to get to the iPod itself.)

People worked to ship the products of his company. Men and women labored to write and produce commercial advertisements to promote the products. Lawyers defended his company's rights in court. His office waste baskets were emptied and his ink cartridges were replaced. Even his dinner was provided for him by people who farmed, cooked, and served.

My point? So many people held positions that were "invisible" and unglamorous. They performed tasks that were "unlovable" and not "delightful." In many cases, I'm sure they didn't love their jobs—they certainly didn't love the paltry wages they earned.

All of these people performed invisible, unglamorous jobs they didn't "love" so that Steve Jobs could follow his dreams and accomplish great things through his company and products.

Don't get me wrong: I don't think that makes Steve Jobs a bad person at all. I don't hold it against him. But facts are facts: Sometimes people don't have jobs they love. Sometimes they have to perform task that aren't necessarily delightful. But they are necessary.

Like it or not, our society depends on people taking unglamorous jobs. Those jobs can include things like bringing in the harvest, transporting food to the grocery stores, repairing a broke water main, fixing a leaking roof or toilet, cleaning bed pans, or walking a guard post at some military base overseas.

I heard recently that a college professor had been working with undergraduates, and he said that many of them are now questioning the "do what you love, love what you do" philosophy of Steve Jobs. This same professor often tells them a story about his dad. His dad didn't love what he did. His dad did a job that he despised in order to put three children through college.

Earlier in his life, the professor wondered if his dad was mistaken in thinking that it was important to put the needs of other people before his own personal needs. His dad made necessity into a virtue. He acted as if taking the best care you can of your family is a form of self-service.

When I thought about it, it occurred to me that people like Mother Teresa, Nelson Mandela, and Martin Luther King, Jr. didn't organize their lives around a bucket list. They found meaning in their heroic self-sacrifice. But they didn't do what they did in order to achieve meaning or significance. They did it because, like the professor's dad, it needed to be done. They felt they had to do it.

Sometimes we can't do what we want to do. Sometimes we simply have to do what needs to be done. It may not be our passion. It may be boring, in fact. For the sake of others, we may have to sacrifice our self-fulfillment. That's the attitude that Jesus took. It wasn't his pursuit of self-satisfaction that led him to be nailed to the cross. It was total commitment to self-sacrifice. And that's the same attitude that we should be willing to adopt as his disciples. We are called to be servants of others—to intentionally seek the happiness and the self-fulfillment of other people rather than ourselves, regardless of the costs. It is only in denying ourselves in the imitation of Christ that we can ever experience the true depths of our faith. If we embrace His compassion and His humility, we can be led by the Spirit of God to transform the world we live in. It is by taking up the cross, not commiting to "do what we love," that we will find the greatest peace and joy. For we will be like Jesus and will enjoy union of heart and mind with him.

OUR DEEPEST DESIRE

Saint Augustine claimed that the inner hunger that all of us feel is, in truth, a desire to be united, or reunited, with our Creator. This yearning is of a kind that no worldly possession or human being could possibly satisfy, and it would not have been implanted in us if it could not be gratified in some other way. Why would God implant this craving within our souls? To draw us closer to Him.

So I continued my weekly routine of driving an hour and forty-five minutes to work, flying a three or four-day trip, then returning home. Over the years, my wife and children faithfully attended Sunday Mass, but because my work schedule had me working on week-ends, I had fallen away from my weekly attendance. When I realized that very soon, we would be facing an "empty nest" situation, I found myself looking ahead to an uncertain future. I knew there was more to life than what I was experiencing and after some wise advice from a priest, I decided to "get spiritual."

BRUSH WITH DEATH

Another life-changing event occurred in the spring of 1995 when I was in Houston for flight- training. This training cycle was to last around sixty days, for most of which I would remain in Houston. After about fifty days of being there, I was in the phase of flight sim-ulator training. This was fast-paced and demanding. I was paired with Captain Steve Rhule, who became my "guardian angel." After an afternoon simulator session, we went out to dinner and agreed to meet that evening to go over our next day's simulator session. We met that evening but ended early because we had an early show at 5:30 in the next morning.

Around 2:30 in the morning, I woke up and had an urge to use the bathroom. My discharge looked like black tar. I assumed it was just the result of my earlier dinner and returned to my bed. I had the same urge two more times that night, with the same results, and after the third time, I couldn't stand up. I became dizzy and weak when I tried to stand.

I knew that I wouldn't be physically or psychologically ready for the morning simulator session. I crawled back to my bed and called my simulator partner, Captain Rhule, to tell him of my condition and inform him that I would not be able to be his simulator partner that morning.

"Don't worry," he said. "I'll be right over."

I insisted that he shouldn't come over, because I couldn't unlock the hotel door. But he wasn't deterred. About two minutes later, he was knocking on my door.

"I can't get to the door," I said.

He called the hotel maintenance person to unlock my door. But I also had the chain lock engaged on the door, and the maintenance person was unable to remove it.

"I'm calling the fire department," Captain Rhule said, over my protests.

I decided to crawl over to the door. With great effort, I was able to unlock it. The fire department and emergency personnel rushed in and began evaluating my condition. Their initial diagnosis was that I was having a diabetic seizure, but discounted that after checking my blood sugar. I was whisked into the ambulance and taken to the Houston Medical Center's Emergency Room. Captain Rhule accompanied me in the ambulance, but once I was in the emergency room, they kicked him out.

I actually felt pretty good and was in the process of telling that to the emergency room doctor when I passed out. When I woke-up I had doctors and nurses surrounding me. Apparently I had a tremendous discharge of blood from my rectum, and the doctor was trying to insert a tube into my nose and extend that tube down into my stomach. Once the tube reached my throat, I started gagging, and I pulled the tube out from my nose.

After doing this two more times, the doctor informed me that if I did it again, he was going to tie my hands. He sprayed my throat with something and this time was able to successfully insert the tube into my stomach. They took me into the operating room, and when I woke from the surgery, the doctor's words shocked me.

"You're lucky to be alive," he said.

"What do you mean?" I asked.

He told me that I had two bleeding ulcers, and that I had almost bled to death. If I had remained in my hotel room for just five more minutes, I would have bled to death. I will always be indebted to Captain Rhule for his quick action. (Captain Rhule passed away in 2013 from a massive heart attack, three years after he retired. God rest his soul.)

DISCERNMENT

After this "near death" experience, I decided to re-evaluate my life. For me, that meant returning to full

Communion in the Catholic Church. So in the fall of 1995, I made a conscious effort to arrange my schedule so that on Sundays I could attend Mass at my location.

I began to embrace the sacramental life of the Church. I noticed my heart was changing. Over the next several years, I had moved up in seniority, which enabled me to have weekends off. I started to become active in the parish, serving in ministry and getting involved in various Church activities and functions. In 1997, after Sunday Mass, I again heard about an invitation to look into the permanent deacon program in the diocese. I really didn't say anything to my wife this time because (as I wrote earlier) several years before she told me that she wouldn't be interested in accompanying me in this journey.

After the presentation was completed, we left the church and decided to go out for breakfast. While driving to the restaurant, my wife said to me, "You know dear, if you're still interested in becoming a deacon, I think you should check into it." I have no doubt that invitation from my wife had come from the Holy Spirit. I prayed before the Blessed Sacrament to make sure this calling was from God. I think I was starting to get scared and maybe trying to dismiss it and convince myself I was making a mistake; but the next morning I didn't feel scared. Instead, I had the feeling, along with other signs, that I really had to say "yes." So, with confidence and exhilaration and my wife Lynn's blessing, I applied and was accepted into the Erie Diocese deacon formation program.

HONORED TO BE ORDAINED

After four challenging years of formation, I had the unbelievable privilege of being ordained as a Permanent Deacon of the Diocese of Erie. It was "Good News" and seemed too good to be true, but my life was making sense now. I was more engaged and doing more for the Church which not only helped the Church but helped our marriage. Flying was no longer a major part of my life. When I would be introduced to someone and they asked me what I did, I would say I was a Permanent Deacon for the Diocese of Erie. I would even say that when I was in my pilot's uniform. For years, I was proud to be identified as a captain for a major airline; after ordination, my priorities shifted.

ANOTHER CLOSE CALL

After my ordination in 2002, I did continue to fly. Inevitably, when someone found out that I was an airline pilot they would ask me many questions. Here are just a few that are asked the most:

- Did you ever have a scary moment while flying?

- Are planes really safer than cars?

- Can you sleep during the flight?

- Have you ever crashed?

In my twenty-six-year career as a professional airline pilot and my twenty years as a general aviation pilot, I never crashed or had an incident with an aircraft. That is, until November 23rd, 2010, when I was flying from Houston, Texas (IAH) to Mexico City (MEX) in a Boeing 737.

It started out like a typical international flight. It was the third day of a four-day pairing. We departed the gate in Houston (IAH) 0301Z (9:01pm) with a full plane. Every seat was filled. The weather condition in IAH was night FVR (partly cloudy skies) in both Houston and Mexico City. The flight time was scheduled for one hour and fifty-eight minutes. The take-off, climb, and cruise were uneventful.

Approximately twenty minutes before we began our descent —into Mexico City (MEX), I did a thorough brief of the B737 Mateo Transition Approach to

Runway 05-Right, which included covering Notices to Airmen (NOTAM's). These are time-critical in nature and would affect a pilot's decision to make a flight. NOTAMs include such things as an inoperative navigation facility, a closed airport, or restrictions on en route navigation aids.

There are also terrain considerations, along with a review of the standard terminal arrival routes (STARs), which are designed primarily for high performance turbine aircraft. All Minimum Obstruction Clearance Altitude (MORA's) which assures a reliable navigation signal, Minimum Enroute Altitude (MEA's,) are the lowest altitude that a pilot could fly, the Minimum Obstruction Clearance Altitude (MOCA's) is the altitude which guarantees the same terrain clearance as the Minimum Enroute Altitude (MEA) but the MOCA assures a reliable navigation signal only within 22 nautical miles of the navigation facility, while the MEA guarantees reliable navigation signals throughout the course, and the instrument approach to runway 05-Left.

We began our descent and completed the in-range checklist and everything was going just fine. We then accomplished the approach checklist and were cleared for the ILS-05R approach Mateo Transition. Approximately nine miles from SMO (Mateo) VOR, Mexico City approach suddenly gave us radar vectors "off" the approach.

"Why?" I asked them.

The people at Mexico City approach responded that it was due to traffic.

While on the assigned heading, we were then given holding instructions. We were told to hold at Lucia VOR at 12,000 feet. That was it. I wasn't given the normal and required EFC (Expect Further Clearance) time. We were scrambling to locate the holding fix and once we did, we were only four miles from the fix. Crew resources management (CRM) worked very well and we were able to enter the hold. After only about forty seconds into the hold we were given instructions to exit the hold and given a heading to intercept a radial off of the SMO VOR. I asked the controller what their intentions were after that.

They informed me that we had now been cleared for the VOR DME Rwy 05L approach into Mexico City and to descend to 10,000 feet and slow to 160 knots. At that point we were only about 6 miles from the SMO VOR. The workload in the cockpit was manageable only because of good CRM. We now briefed for another approach to a different runway and descended to 9,700 feet as per the approach instructions.

According to Mexico City approach we were following an MD-80. Suddenly, without any warning, the aircraft violently and immediately banked to the left and kept going, past 95+ degrees. We both heard the audio warning "bank-angle" and both of us had our hands on the yoke trying to stop and reverse the roll and stabilize the aircraft. I picked-up the mic.

"We've encountered extreme turbulence," I told approach. "Are we following another aircraft?"

They responded by telling us that we were behind a "heavy' MD-11 which was three miles ahead of us. We continued the approach and landed safely.

I truly believe that if the landing gear had not been extended, the aircraft would have barrel rolled. When I opened the cockpit door, it was only then that I realized how violent the turbulence was, when not one of the passengers had departed the aircraft. Many were crying and, in Spanish, asking the flight attendants what had happened. The Spanish speaking flight attendant later told me that they were very grateful for being safely on the ground.

Several days after this near disaster, I received a call from the Vice President of Operations.

"How are you doing?" he asked me.

"Fine," I said. "What's up?"

He told me that engineering had reviewed and analyzed the Flight Operational Quality Assurance (FOQA) data from the airplane that we were flying into Mexico City and found that my aircraft had exceeded several G-force parameters the aircraft was designed and certified for.

"We're amazed that the airplane survived that turbulent encounter," he said. "We can't explain how you survived that encounter," he repeated. "You are a very lucky man."

After that incident, I decided that I needed to reorganize my priorities and evaluate whether I wanted to continue flying. Philosophically, I believe that life is a journey. In the transportation business, you're always thinking about where you're going more than where you've been. I really don't care where I go. I just like helping people.

MY REAL CALLING

I felt it was time to fully embrace my spiritual journey as a permanent deacon. I believe that journey begins, not when you realize how much you love God, but how much God loves you. I was happy during my flying career, but after experiencing that dangerous incident, I was not happy being an airline pilot anymore. I retired from Continental (United) Airlines a year later.

Just as I got questions about my job as an airline pilot, I also receive questions from friends, family and parishioners who ask me, "What do deacons do?"

I tell them that deacons do all that the church asks of them. The Second Vatican Council never intended to define the functions of deacons, but it did point out the areas of their ministry. Those areas are service in liturgy, word, and charity. Those are three ministries in the church in which we all share by our baptism: responsibility for the unity of the church, responsibility to and for the Word of God, and responsibility to serve others. Because these ministries pertain to all of us by virtue of our baptism, however, there is a need that someone, somewhere, personify these ministries in an ordained fashion, as a concrete sign to us all and as a remembrance of our share in these ministries. The one responsible for the special ministry of service to others is the deacon.

As Pope Francis put it when he proclaimed 2016 to be a Holy Year of Mercy, "All consolation is rooted in the warmth of God's embrace." That's true. Whatever success I've had in my career, whatever meaning my life has had, it is only because of the warm embrace of God's love. Over my twenty-six year airline career and my twelve years as a deacon, I have learned that sharing faith empowers faith. I have also learned—quite well—that I am just a vessel meant to be used by God. I am committed to finishing the task God has called me to. But even as I write that, I know that it is "not I, but Christ" who is doing the work in me (Galatians 2:20). He is the one who will complete the good work that he has ordained for me. Simply put, he's the master and I'm the servant. I just do what I do and try to bring faith to the people I meet.

Christ's message to me was one of service: first as a pilot, then later—and now—as a deacon. In order for us to love one another, we must connect with others and find our true selves reflected in them—by putting them and their needs before ours. That's how I try to "be all I can be."

CONCLUSION

Some Final Remarks About the Seats I've Occupied

This memoir has been about my spiritual journey—about the three seats I've occupied in life. But ultimately, I hope my story is not really even about me. It should be about God and about you.

ON A WING: MY PILOT SEAT

Flying has been a part of my life since I was two years old. It is a very individual and personal experience. Being an airline pilot was a career that inspired me to work in the face of many unique and unusual challenges. I am so grateful for all the experiences and lessons that my life in the sky has provided me.

AND A PRAYER: MY DEACON SEAT

As you know by now, on April 26th, 2002 I became a Permanent Deacon of the Diocese of Erie. Deacons are not primarily needed because of any unique shortage of priests or because of any unique set of roles deacons might perform, but because the church needed a permanent sacramental sign of her own diaconal nature. The truth is that as a deacon I have no authority (power). God has the authority (power). God is acting in our words and gestures and is present in the generosity and kindness we offer. It has been a triumphant privilege to serve as a sign of God's authority—and I hope that this simple testimony of my spiritual journey can be an extension of my service as a Deacon, to help others experience the "warm embrace" of God's love that Pope Francis talked about.

THE SEAT OF SUFFERING...
AS A BROKEN HUMAN BEING

Finally, as I've said, I've sat in a seat of suffering. Like many of you, I know what it means to be a broken human being.

In John 5:17-30, Jesus talks about how the Father is at work in the world, and he says something that startles those who first hear it. First, he claims equality with God the Father:

> *"My Father is at work until now, so I am at work.*
> *For this reason they tried all the more to kill him,*
> *Because he not only broke the Sabbath*
> *But he also called God his own father,*
> *Making himself equal to God."*

113

Pretty amazing! Scandalous to the people at the time. But perhaps just as surprising is that Jesus says something about his relationship with the Father:

Jesus answered and said to them, "Amen, amen, I say to you, the Son cannot do anything on his own."

The two things that I take out of that passage are this: first, that since Jesus is equal to God, there's no one better I can trust. Throughout my life, he is the one who has sustained me in my suffering, offered mercy to me in my failures, and steadied me when my life was spinning out of control.

Are there some days in your life when you wish that God would move right in and take over for a while? Those times are when things are going hay-wire. And yet, the crazy thing I have learned (from learning the hard way) is that even when life is tough and turbulent, we resist turning the controls over to Jesus. Ironically, we are worried that we might lose control. We don't realize that it is trying to control our lives that really puts us out of control! That's when we need to think about what Jesus said in the passage that I just quoted: "The son cannot do anything on his own."

If Jesus who is equal with God never did anything on his own, independent of his Father, why do we think we can? With all that I have experienced and endured, viewing life from my seat of suffering, I have definitely learned that I cannot do anything on my own!

You've seen those great bumper stickers that say, "Jesus is my co-pilot," right? Well, I used to think those were pretty neat. I loved the sentiment. Then one day I heard someone make a great point. Jesus shouldn't be your co-pilot. He should be your pilot! Yes, that's absolutely right. Jesus should be at the controls. He should be in the seat of authority in your heart and life. When he is, your life—your flight of faith, I might say—will be one that glorifies God.

ABOUT THE AUTHOR

Dennis Kudlak was ordained a Deacon of the Catholic Church in 2002 and serves the Diocese of Erie, Pennsylvania. A graduate of Gannon College (now Gannon University), Dennis earned a Bachelors of Business Management, and in 2013 graduate theological education at the Lexington Theological Seminary (MAPM). He went on to serve twenty-six years as a commercial pilot for Continental Airlines; graduating from Flight Engineering School in 1988, attaining the rank of Captain in 1997, and retiring in 2014. He and his wife, Lynn, are the parents of four grown children. In his spare time, Deacon Kudlak enjoys boating, fishing, meditation, and spending time with his grandchildren. Find him online at **dennismkudlak.com**.

INVITE DEACON DENNIS TO SPEAK

Deacon Dennis Kudlak regularly speaks to various groups about the Catholic faith and how God has worked in his own life. He not only enjoys delivering homilies in his role as deacon, but loves to encourage others by sharing how God makes himself present to us in the midst of the ups and downs of our lives.

If your parish, ministry, or non-profit group would like to invite Deacon Dennis Kudlak to speak at an event, please visit **www.dennismkudlak.com** or email him directly at **deaconden@roadrunner.com**.

SUGGESTED
SPIRITUAL READINGS

Deacon Dennis believes this books will minister to your soul and help you through tough times:

- *The Humility and Suffering of God* by Francois Varillon

- *On the Christian Meaning of Human Suffering (Salvifici Dolores)* by Pope Saint John Paul II

- *Making Sense Out of Suffering* by Peter Kreeft

- *The Holy Longing: The Search for Christian Spirituality* by Ronald Rolheiser

All of these books can be found at Amazon.com, Barnes and Noble.com, or ordered at virtually any retail book store.

31910705R00081

Made in the USA
Middletown, DE
16 May 2016